YOU CAN'T
TEXT
A TOUGH
CONVERSATION

Other Books by Mike Bechtle

Evangelism for the Rest of Us
How to Communicate with Confidence
People Can't Drive You Crazy if You Don't Give Them the Keys

YOU CAN'T
TEXT
A TOUGH
CONVERSATION

#RealCommunicationNeeded

DR. MIKE BECHTLE

Revell

a division of Baker Publishing Group
www.RevellBooks.com

Published by Revell
a division of Baker Publishing Group
P.O. Box 6287, Grand Rapids, MI 49516-6287
www.revellbooks.com

Printed in the United States of America

Library of Congress Cataloging-in-Publication Data
Bechtle, Mike, 1952–
    You can't text a tough conversation : #realcommunicationneeded / Mike Bechtle.
        pages cm
    Includes bibliographical references.
    ISBN 978-0-8007-2382-8 (pbk.)
    1. Conversation—Religious aspects—Christianity. 2. Oral communication—Religious aspects—Christianity. 3. Text messaging (Cell phone systems). I. Title.
    BV4597.53.C64B43 2015
    153.6—dc23   2015015855

Published in association with the literary agency of Alive Communications, Inc., 7680 Goddard Street, Suite 200, Colorado Springs, CO 80920, www.alivecommunications.com.

In keeping with biblical principles of creation stewardship, Baker Publishing Group advocates the responsible use of our natural resources. As a member of the Green Press Initiative, our company uses recycled paper when possible. The text paper of this book is composed in part of post-consumer waste.

15 16 17 18 19 20 21   7 6 5 4 3 2 1

To Brian
Every dad's dream is to have his daughter
marry a man of character.
You fulfilled that dream,
and I'm grateful you're in her life—
and mine.

Contents

Acknowledgments

When I wrote my first book, I realized that there are a lot of people who are involved in making it happen. Some (like editors and agents) are directly involved. Others (like a spouse) come alongside your dream and believe in you. Others are impacted by the fact that you're spending time with a manuscript you might normally be spending with them.

It's all still true.

Vicki Crumpton has been my editor for all four of my books. It's been like having a personal coach and mentor who comes alongside and teaches you how to get better each time. She uses up a lot of red ink on my manuscripts, which means that any success this book achieves has her fingerprints all over it. Working with her has been one of the main reasons I've come to love writing. She's as good as they get. Thanks, Coach!

Somewhere along the line, Joel Kneedler shifted from being my agent to being my friend. He guided the initial decisions for my last book and this one and has helped steer my writing career over the past few years. He's moved on to the next level in the publishing world, but I'm grateful for his belief in me when I wasn't sure which way to go next. Thanks for the partnership!

My wife, Diane, was more heavily involved in this book than any other. Her input on the content and her comments on the manuscript shaped my ideas in priceless ways. Those discussions had the potential to turn into "tough conversations," but she found the balance between being tough and tender. You've always been my biggest fan, and I'll always be yours. I'm grateful for you just being you!

Finally, there are the people I have coffee or hang out with, and that hasn't happened as much over the past few months. Sara, Tim, Brian, my grandkids, and my new daughter-in-law, Lucy, deserve more focus in the coming weeks as soon as I hit "send" and this book goes on its way. You guys are all priceless gifts to me, and I love you.

Then there's God. What can I say? Eternally grateful . . .

Introduction

What We've Got Here Is a Failure to Communicate

Some people can't sleep because they have insomnia.
I can't sleep because I have internet.

Anonymous

D o you want to know what your communication will be like in your marriage?" the counselor asked.

We were young and in love. Like most couples, Diane and I knew our marriage would be different. We had seen other people fall in love, get married with high expectations, but then spiral downward over time. They started fighting or withdrawing from each other, and the marital magic disappeared in the first few years.

We knew that wouldn't happen to us. We had something special between us, and it would carry us through to sheer bliss. Sure, we'd have struggles. But we were in l-o-v-e, and we believed that our unique passion for each other would help us calmly negotiate those issues, find quick solutions, and make us even stronger.

"Sure," we replied to the counselor, convinced we knew the answer. We had gone through several sessions of premarital counseling with him already, and his guidance was always spot on. "What's our communication going to be like?"

"Well, it's not a foolproof technique," he continued. "But here's the best predictor of what your communication will be like. Imagine what it would be like if Mike's dad was married to Diane's mom."

It took a few minutes for Diane to regain consciousness while I picked my jaw up off the floor. That wasn't what we expected to hear. Our first reaction was, "But that's not fair. We're not our parents. We're our own people. We've learned from their mistakes."

He went on to explain. "Like I said, it's not foolproof. But no matter what our parents tried to teach us, we learned how to communicate by watching how they did it. We subconsciously believe actions more than words, and we develop a default setting by observing them over time. Sure, we can work around it," he said. "We can learn new ways of communicating, and we can make intentional choices to do it differently. But when we're under pressure and emotions are high, our 'chooser' muscles quit working. We drop back to our default settings. We respond the way our parents did."

Diane and I had some long conversations after that appointment. Decades later, we've found it to be true. I'm not my dad, and Diane's not her mom. We've made a lot of choices to become our own persons. But their fingerprints are all over us.

Tough Talking

We learn by watching more than listening. We hear words, but we absorb actions. The life lessons we learn come by seeing how the key people in our lives respond to what life brings them. No matter what they say, we see their true character when things get tough and they're under pressure and their defenses are down.

This is true not just in marital communication. I remember walking into my daughter's room when she was a toddler and watching how she was disciplining her dolls. She wasn't using the kind, logical techniques we had tried to use with her. She was using the techniques we used when we were upset.

Ouch.

We learned how to communicate with others by observing the people who raised us. It doesn't matter if we had a single parent, two parents, multiple custody situations, foster homes, or a dysfunctional setting. We learned to negotiate life by watching how people in that role interacted with others—spouses, siblings, friends, bosses, and strangers. That's how we built the communication toolbox that we use in our lives and relationships.

When relationships get challenging and conversations get tough, we use whatever default tools we have. We usually don't stop to question their effectiveness, because they're familiar. When they don't work well, we just try to use more force or pressure. It's like using a pencil eraser to get rid of something written in ink. It doesn't work well, but it's all we have—so we either rub harder or give up in frustration.

But we can get new tools and techniques. We don't have to be stuck with our default settings. We can develop new patterns of communicating that are effective in the toughest conversations.

Our kids are in their thirties now, and we see ourselves in them—both the good stuff and the bad stuff. But we also see who they've become by the choices they've made. They aren't us. They recognized the healthy patterns they saw and adapted them. They still have the tools they picked up from us, but they learned which ones are more effective than others, and they got new tools on their own to replace the ineffective ones.

The Wild Card

There are dozens, if not hundreds, of books on how to communicate effectively. Many people have been helped by these books, and they provide resources to strengthen relationships. I recommend many of them to my clients on a regular basis.

But a wild card has appeared that wasn't present when some of those classic books were written: technology.

Technology has been around for a long time, and we've used it as a tool to communicate more rapidly and effectively. But in the past few years, technology has moved from *enhancing* conversation to *replacing* conversation. People send messages back and forth, not realizing that they never have live contact with the other person. It's not unusual for people to connect electronically with someone for months or even years without having a real conversation. (I bet you can think of someone right now whom you frequently communicate with through social media but with whom you haven't had a live conversation in years.)

"That's okay, right?" one might ask. "We're still communicating. The relationship looks a little different, but we're still connecting back and forth. What's wrong with that?"

One study showed that only 7 percent of communication is the words we use. Thirty-eight percent is our tone of voice, and 55 percent is body language.[1]

In face-to-face conversation, we're using all three. On the phone, we've lost the body language—so we're down to two. When our communication is completely through email, texting, or social media, we're down to one—and we've lost 93 percent of the tools that help us connect.

Early one morning, I was greeted by the training director of a large entertainment company. I had worked with her a number of times in the past. As I set up for class, we chatted about her thirty-plus years with the corporation and how she rose through the ranks to reach her current position. I started the session, and she went back to her office.

We broke for lunch, and the participants wandered out of the room. The training director walked in, and her face looked like she had seen a ghost. "What's wrong?" I asked.

"I just got laid off."

"Seriously?" I said. "And you didn't know it was coming? Who told you?"

"Someone sent me an email."

As it turned out, the decision to terminate her had come from someone much younger than her. Evidently, because he was so comfortable with communication through technology, he assumed there wouldn't be anything wrong with letting her go without a face-to-face conversation.

I don't know how things turned out, because it was the last time I saw her. But I've thought about that situation often since then. I'm guessing he probably got in trouble for that approach, and the training director might have had some recourse. It demonstrated to me that technology has its limitations, one of which is when people use it to avoid having a difficult conversation.

Time for a Change

In general, people have gotten worse at conversation while they've gotten better at technology. Everybody communicates. But when people communicate electronically, they're not communicating in person.

Is that a problem or not?

People are talking less and texting more. That works for casual conversation, but it's difficult to have tough conversations in writing alone. Unfortunately, people do it all the time, and relationships get damaged in the process. If we think electronic communication is just as effective as face-to-face communication, we'll assume that it's just as effective for tough conversations as for casual ones.

That's a dangerous assumption. It's like having a phone conversation in which one person loses their cellular signal and gets cut off. But the other person keeps talking, unaware that nobody is hearing what they say.

This book is designed to help us build a strategy for effective conversation in a digital world:

- We'll learn the value of face-to-face conversation.
- We'll see that being genuine is better than appearing perfect electronically.
- We'll discover the basics of effective communication, building on the principles that grow effective relationships.
- We'll identify the six tools needed to navigate tough conversations.
- We'll explore six skills for using those tools to make conversation genuine.
- We'll develop a sense for when it's time to apply those tools and skills and how to do preventative maintenance to keep our relationships healthy.
- We'll learn how to use technology instead of being used by it.

With the right tools and skills, we can learn to negotiate the toughest conversations without intimidation or frustration. We can learn to communicate with:

- the spouse who withdraws and won't engage
- the teenager who turns every conversation into a battle

- the in-laws who overstep their boundaries
- the friends who can't stop giving advice
- the neighbors who won't trim their tree that hangs over our fence and drops leaves in our yard
- the church member who expects us to perform in a certain way
- the co-worker in the next cubicle who goes out of his way to be sarcastic
- the boss who criticizes everything we do

We'll also talk about the conversational issues that keep genuine communication from taking place—from the elephant in the room that nobody talks about to the emotion that keeps us from genuine connection.

Starting the Journey

Effective communication is the key to healthy relationships, both personal and professional. We're not just working on our skills so people will be impressed with our conversational abilities. We do it because we care about these relationships and the people in them.

If we want healthy relationships, we need healthy communication. With a little direction and a little intentional effort, we can move our communication to the next level. We're not stuck with our default settings. We can get new tools and learn how to use them well.

We don't mind investing time and money to improve our golf swing, develop a hobby, or work on our fitness. Isn't it time to make an investment in our communication skills?

The return on that investment will last a lifetime.

PART 1

The Process of Conversation

When I want to learn how to do something, I find a book on the topic. I read the book, gain as much knowledge as I can, and then try to do it. I am usually successful, but it can take a long time.

If I had a leaky faucet, for example, I would pick up a book on do-it-yourself plumbing. I'd read about how faucets work. Then I'd study the different types of faucets. I would read about what causes leaks and the most common ways to fix those leaks. Then I would make sure I had the right tools and start working on the faucet. With the book in one hand and a wrench in the other, I would start taking the faucet apart. After each step, I'd check the book to make sure I had done it correctly and to familiarize myself with the next step.

Then I met my father-in-law. When he wanted to fix something, he didn't read a book. He grabbed some tools and started dismantling it. He would figure it out by looking and experimenting. In almost every case, he identified what needed to be done—and it took a lot less time than my approach.

They were a waterskiing family. So when I married his daughter, he taught me how to water-ski. "Don't you dare go get a book on waterskiing," he said. "I'm going to hand you a rope and push you off the back of the boat. You better hang on." And I quickly learned how to ski.

I've gotten much better over the years. I still like to read about things, but I've learned the value of just starting on something.

Relationships require the ability to do both. They're complicated and messy, and they don't come with instructions. Books can help with understanding them, but we have to jump in and do the hard work of growing those relationships.

So let's start with the book work. This section explores how relationships and communication work at the most basic level. Once we lay that foundation, we'll get the tools we need and learn the skills of building relationships that thrive instead of just survive.

1

How the Elephant Got in the Room

When there's an elephant in the room, introduce him.

Randy Pausch[1]

My daughter, Sara, asked me if I could build her a certain piece of furniture. I said, "Of course." In fact, I gave her a certificate for it for Christmas.

Two years ago.

The problem was that I didn't know how I was going to build it. I do well with plans but not with making things up. This project didn't have plans. I would think about how to do it but couldn't figure it out. So I would set it aside for a couple of weeks, thinking it would percolate in the background and I'd know what to do.

A week or two later, nothing had changed. I wasn't any closer to a solution. So I kept putting it off week after week, month after month—because I was stumped. When I don't know how to do something, my default setting is to procrastinate instead of jumping in and tackling it.

Whenever Sara and I would talk, I would carefully avoid the subject. I didn't want to let her down or appear incompetent. Since we weren't talking about it, she didn't know what was happening. I assumed she was either irritated with or disappointed in me. But I never asked, so I never knew for sure. I think I was afraid to ask.

Eventually, I realized the situation had created an unspoken barrier between us. My daughter is one of the people I enjoy talking to the most on the planet, and I want a close, loving relationship with her. But my silence was building an unspoken wall that had been growing for two years.

Once I figured out what was happening, I went to her and told her what I was feeling. I apologized, wanting to do my part to remove the barrier I had created.

As we talked, she said, "Yeah, it was the elephant in the room."

That's a word picture we've all heard and experienced. An elephant is in the room when something obvious is going on and nobody talks about it, and we pretend it's not there.

I pictured the scenario. I'm sitting on one side of the living room, and my daughter is on the other side. We're peering through the elephant's legs, trying to make conversation. The elephant smells, and it fills the room. It's noisy. It's huge. But we don't talk about it.

Once we acknowledge it, we think, "How in the world did that huge elephant get in this room? It doesn't even fit through the door!"

Sound familiar? Is there anyone in your life with whom you share an elephant—something that everybody knows about but nobody talks about? Nobody wants to say anything, because it will be uncomfortable and people might get upset. The longer the elephant has been there, the harder it is to talk about. But it's big, and it smells. It gets in the way of genuine relationships taking place.

So how *did* that huge elephant get into the room?

It came in when it was little.

If we had talked about it when it first entered, we could simply have guided it out through the door. But when we let it stay, it grew and grew and grew. Getting rid of it became a much bigger issue. Once an elephant becomes full-grown, we might need to remove some walls and get professional help to be rid of it.

When I finally acknowledged the elephant with my daughter, she said, "You know, if you had told me you couldn't figure it out, we could have spent a day working together on it until we knew what to do." That would have been an awesome day with her. One of our favorite dates is to get coffee at Starbucks and cruise around a hardware store or lumberyard.

I love my daughter. And I love the fact that we got rid of the elephant. She loves the fact that I finished the furniture. And the house doesn't smell like elephant anymore.

What's the lesson? Watch for baby elephants in the room. If you let them stay, they'll get really, really big.

Elephant Prevention

Part of the problem is that we get used to having the elephant around. We don't talk about it, and it becomes easier to ignore over time. We don't notice that it's growing, because it happens slowly. It's like when someone hasn't seen our kids for six months, and they're amazed at how much the kids have grown. We don't notice the growth because it has been so gradual. But to anyone else, it's obvious.

Toxic communication patterns in our relationships also start slowly, and we don't want to talk about them. They're uncomfortable. After a while, we get used to those patterns and they seem normal. It's like mold growing behind our walls. If we don't do the hard work of dealing with the patterns, our relationship could be in jeopardy.

Nobody likes tough conversations. They're not nearly as much fun as easy conversations. But they're the key to keeping the elephants out of the room. If the elephants are already big, it's going to take significantly more work to remove them, and the conversations could be painful.

The best approach is to have the tough conversations when the elephant is little. Someone has to have the courage to identify the elephant and start talking about it.

Too often, people see the elephant and start blaming each other for letting it in the room. They work against each other instead of working together to solve the problem. Meanwhile, the elephant wanders around the room fluffing the pillows and deciding where to sleep.

We get in trouble when we see each other as the problem instead of the elephant.

Handcrafted Relationships

My father-in-law is a master woodworker. Each of his three daughters' homes contains pieces of furniture, cabinetry, and design elements that express his love and creativity. When our kids were growing up and needed something for their room, their first thought was always, "Grandpa could build that for me." He usually did, and they loved it.

His specialty has become turned segmented wooden bowls. In what seems like a geometric impossibility, he cuts hundreds of small pieces of exotic hardwoods at precise angles, glues them together, and makes museum-quality bowls in which every seam of the intricate design matches perfectly.

A few months ago, I was leading a seminar in Honolulu. One evening, I saw turned segmented bowls in a gallery in a high-end shopping center. They looked great but didn't match the quality my father-in-law produces.

I've done some woodworking and might be able to make a simple bowl. To the average person, it might look like any other bowl. But to someone who knows quality, it wouldn't compare to the ones my father-in-law makes. He's spent his life paying his dues to perfect his skills. I haven't. True quality takes time. When things are mass-produced, they cost a lot less than things that are handcrafted, but they aren't as good.

Relationships are the same way. Good ones take time and work. When we get a new boss or co-worker, make a new friend or move into a new neighborhood, we form new relationships. They might feel strong at the beginning, and the connections are energizing. But the longer those relationships continue, the more challenges they face. For some relationships, those challenges pull them apart and the relationship ends. But for others, the challenges draw them together, becoming the building blocks for relationships that endure.

Relationships take work. If there's tension with a cubicle partner, it drains our energy at work. An unreasonable teacher or classmate can make a semester seem like an eternity. A strained relationship with a landlord or tenant is like a black cloud that hangs over the relationship.

The more important a relationship is to us, the more work it takes. That work takes place through communication. The longer a relationship continues, the more challenging the communication becomes, and it's easy to find an elephant in the living room and wonder when it arrived. Knowing the stages a relationship goes through can provide clues to elephant prevention.

There are eight stages that relationships go through as they mature. These stages look different in different types of relationships, so they need to be adapted to each situation. But the basic process is the same.

Let's see how this applies to a typical couple. Their relationship might progress like this:

1. *Attraction.* Two people catch each other's attention. Something about the way the other looks, talks, or acts produces the first spark of interest. (These first impressions take place in every connection, from a dating relationship to a job interview.)

2. *Approach.* That interest leads them to connect with each other, usually in some type of conversation. They find something they experience together to talk about, whether it's the event they're attending, the environment, or some other common ground.

3. *Admiration.* During the conversation, they use that common ground to explore other possibilities of mutual interest. The more they discover about each other, the more they want to keep discovering. So they set up future times to connect.

4. *Attention.* The couple enjoys being together, so they look for opportunities to be together more often. Each is on their best behavior, trying to impress the other person. Eventually, they commit to a relationship.

5. *Accommodation.* The relationship grows, and they focus on making each other happy. Most of their conversations have been about the things they have in common. But over time, their uniqueness comes out, and they have to explore their differences. That can lead to some uncomfortable conversations, but their commitment to each other drives them to find solutions.

6. *Anticipation.* After the wedding, they ride their high emotions as they begin their life together. They're excited, and they're happy. Sure, they have lots of little disagreements, but they're so much in love that they find ways to work through

them. The energy of the relationship carries them through the tough times. (This is often when the baby elephant sneaks in. "Love is blind" means that our attention is on the excitement of the relationship, so we're not paying attention to the little stuff that happens around us.)

7. *Apathy.* The relationship grows, but life gets busy. The initial excitement wears off, and daily pressures of work and other commitments begin to grow. Those little disagreements still come up, but there is less romantic energy to work on them. Tackling the tough issues becomes more challenging, and resources are more limited. The little elephant has found his place in the house and settled in.

8. *Arrangement.* At this point, couples begin to form patterns of communicating. Generally, those patterns fall into one of two categories:

1. dealing with the tough issues by talking about them
2. avoiding the tough issues because they're uncomfortable

The first category takes a lot of work. Neither person is an expert, so they're probably at a loss for solutions. But they hang in there and work on the problems, going through the initial discomfort to avoid a lot of pain later. When the pressure comes, they keep it on the outside of their relationship, using it to push them together. They acknowledge the elephant and take steps to send it on its way.

The second category is the path of least resistance. The couple becomes irritated with each other because the problem isn't being dealt with. That irritation grows under the surface, building layer after layer of protection—like an onion growing from the inside out. When the pressure comes, they let that pressure come between them, pushing them apart. Those layers protect them from each other. But they've also protected themselves from seeing the elephant.

The Decision Point

When couples reach this fork in the road, they don't have a road map to figure things out. Sometimes they choose the path of connecting, recognizing the need to work through the tough stuff. But too often they choose the path of disconnecting, because it's an easier path. The elephant doesn't go away; the couple just doesn't talk about it. That's dangerous. If the issues aren't dealt with, they grow. The couple pretends everything is good, but there's a toxic issue growing under the surface.

My nephew and his family live in Minot, North Dakota. The house they were renting was growing mold. They didn't notice it when they first moved in, but over time their health was compromised. They began to develop symptoms of asthma and other issues. The problem was toxic, and it was growing, and they finally had to move out. They had to make the tough choices to deal with the problem so it didn't ruin their lives.

That's what happens in relationships when little issues are ignored; they become big issues. It doesn't matter if it's a work setting or a personal setting. If those issues are not addressed, they can compromise the health of the relationship.

Why We Don't Ask for Help

We might feel like our relationship is perfect. So when the elephant gets bigger and smellier, we don't want to spoil that image. That's exhausting, because it takes a lot of energy to pretend that we're okay when we're not. We're not being honest about the elephant, which means we don't deal with it. We're embarrassed to admit that we need help because we feel shame.

That's why we don't want to make a doctor's appointment until we've lost weight and started exercising regularly. We feel shame and want to solve the problem ourselves to show we're in control. But hiding the problem from others makes it almost impossible for us to get help. We don't talk about it. We sequester the elephant in the bedroom when people visit, trying to convince them that we're okay. But it doesn't work. They can smell that something's not right.

Is There Hope?

A few years ago, I weighed about twenty pounds more than I do now. When my granddaughter, Elena, was just starting to talk, she toddled up to me, poked me in the belly, and said, "Baby?" She knew what pregnant moms looked like and made the association. Not exactly what I wanted to hear, but it was honest.

Maybe we need to be as honest as our kids. They're the ones who will say, "Hey! Did you know there's an elephant in the middle of the room? Wow! It stinks! You should get rid of it."

Here's the thing: It's possible to deal with the elephant. There are some basic principles of communication that help us to do the heavy lifting. But they require action. We can't just hope the situation will get better. We have to make choices and do the work for change to take place.

Healthy relationships will face increasingly greater challenges as they grow. But that's okay, because we will have the resources to handle those tough times. It's like working out with weights. If we're out of shape, we don't start with heavy weight lifting. We start by getting off the couch. We use light weights at first, because that's all our muscles can handle. But as we get stronger, we're able to lift heavier weights. If we tried to lift those weights at the beginning, we'd be sore and risk injury. Little steps begin the journey toward health and fitness.

The One Place We Have Control

We can't force another person to change. We can influence them, but we can't force them. The only person we have control over is ourselves.

As our relationships grow, we can discover how to take responsibility for our actions and our choices, and in the process, we may influence others to change. There are no guarantees, but there are basic principles we can follow to take those first steps toward healthier relationships.

We need to focus on expectancy rather than expectations. Rather than trying to squeeze a relationship into a picture we have in our minds, we need to anticipate the creative masterpiece that can emerge as we paint together. With small, consistent steps, we can start to deal with the issues that divide growing relationships.

There's hope for getting the elephant out of the room.

2

How Conversations Get Tough

Watch your words and hold your tongue; you'll save
yourself a lot of grief.

Proverbs 21:23

When our son, Tim, was about three years old, he touched
a hot barbeque. We were standing in the backyard as
I fired up the grill, getting ready to start dinner. He brought
out the food for me, and we were going to cook together. It
was going to be one of those great father-son bonding times.

At one point, he got too close to the barbeque. "Be careful," I said. "Don't touch the barbeque. If you do, you'll burn
yourself." It couldn't have been more than a second later. He
just couldn't help himself as he reached out his index finger
and touched it. I guess it didn't scar him for life, because now
he has a career managing a restaurant. But he still remembers

touching the barbeque. I'm guessing he's pretty careful at his restaurant when he's in the kitchen.

Nobody likes pain. We go out of our way to avoid it. When we feel it, we move away from it. When we touch a barbeque, we don't say, "Ouch! That hurts. But I think I'll keep my finger here for a while so I can really experience the pain." We pull our finger away and avoid touching it in the future. Hopefully, we learn from the pain. That's a healthy response.

When things hurt, it's a signal that something is wrong. We might try to ignore the pain, hoping it will just go away on its own. We might try to take medication to numb the pain so we don't feel it as strongly. But when pain happens, the best response is to figure out what's causing it. Pain should be a trigger that makes us think, "Okay, there's a problem. Let's work on it."

Athletes understand pain and use it to their advantage. If they're injured, the pain tells them it's time to stop and treat the injury so it doesn't get worse. But if they're trying to get stronger and more competitive, they know there will be a different type of pain as they force their body out of its comfort zone. If they avoid that kind of pain, they never grow. They want to achieve breakthrough performance, so they willingly accept the pain of their workouts to move to the next level.

World-class relationships don't just happen; they take intentional effort. Growing our abilities to communicate effectively involves stretching beyond our comfortable conversations. Sometimes we'll feel pain, but it's the pain of growth. We embrace those tough conversations as necessary steps to stronger relationships.

People Pain

We've all had painful relationships. Maybe they started well, but they got more challenging as the relationships developed.

We used to look forward to long hours of conversation; now we dread the encounters because they often turn out badly.

When conversations get painful, we want to avoid the pain. So we try different strategies to make that happen:

- We avoid the other person so we don't have to talk to them.
- We talk to them, but we avoid the subjects that cause the pain.
- We attack the other person, telling them that they're the problem and they need to change.
- We get defensive.
- We withdraw emotionally.
- We give up.
- We eat cookies. (At least we feel better, right?)

So how did it get hard in the first place?

A brand-new baby doesn't come with communication skills hardwired. She learns by watching those around her and imitating what they do. Parents make exaggerated facial expressions when they talk to her, and she mimics them. (That would be an embarrassing video on social media.) They open their eyes wide; she opens hers in response. They smile at her; she learns to smile back. She's collecting tools she'll use to communicate at the most basic level.

As that baby matures, she notices how the people around her communicate. Whether they're good or bad, those methods are contagious:

- She watches people get angry and yell at each other, so she adds that to her set of tools.
- She sees people withdraw during hard conversations, so she learns that hard conversations are to be avoided.

- She sees people ignore each other while spending time on their smartphone and learns that it's okay to ignore people if there's something more interesting online.

She learns what she observes.

The older she gets, the tougher life gets. As she tries to negotiate relationships, she uses whatever tools she has collected over the years. Some work better than others, but they're the only tools she has. When she interacts with other people who also have limited tool sets, each relationship becomes uniquely challenging.

We use the tools we have, even if it's an incomplete set. When relationships become painful, most people don't have a complete set of tools to work through those issues. They don't like pain, but they don't have the right tool to deal with the situation. And often instead of looking for that tool, they try to ignore the pain, hoping it will just go away.

Communication is how we get ahead in the world. If we don't have the right tools, we're limited in how far we can go.

Three Conversational Categories

Tough conversations happen in a variety of relationships: personal, family, business, public, etc. There are basic principles that apply to all types of relationships, but there are also unique approaches that apply differently to each type.

We can broadly assemble relationships into one of three categories.

Relationships We Choose

We select a spouse or dating partner; we choose our friends; we choose a church or social organization and the relationships that come with it. We might consciously take a job because we want to work for a certain boss, and we select a realtor we trust to sell our home.

The closer these relationships are, the greater attention they deserve. A spouse or friend gets more attention because we've made a long-term commitment to them. The others still deserve focus because we've chosen to work with them, but they might be temporary. When the house is sold or the job ends, the relationship disappears from our radar.

When conversations in this category become challenging, we need to have the best tools and techniques at our fingertips.

Relationships We Encounter

This is a broader category, including people who serve us in stores or restaurants, help-line personnel, strangers we meet in our neighborhood, and business encounters with previously unknown colleagues.

Tough conversations with these people need a different approach. We don't have a long-term commitment, and we don't want to expend the same amount of energy on these people as on those in the first category. There's not as much of a relationship at stake, so we don't nurture these relationships in the same way we nurture relationships we choose.

Relationships We Inherit

This is the largest category and often comes along with the relationships we choose. We pick a spouse, but the in-laws come as part of the package. We choose a school for our kids, but we don't get to choose their teacher. We choose a job, but the crazy co-workers are included like fries come with a hamburger.

This category also includes most members of our family of origin. We don't choose our parents or siblings; we inherit them. There is also the dynamic of relating to adult children or aging parents.

There's a unique set of skills for dealing with these relationships, because having them in our lives is not usually optional. But these people often try to sneak into the first category, demanding the same level of energy and focus that our primary relationships deserve. If we don't give these people what they want, they can drive us crazy.

For this group, we need to set boundaries. Then we need to determine a healthy way of responding when they cross those boundaries.

Dealing with the Conversational Categories

Here is a four-step approach to dealing with all three categories.

Prioritize

Time is limited, and so is our energy. We have only so much to give, and there are plenty of people willing to take. The challenge is to determine each person's category. The closer they are to us, the more attention they deserve.

There's a concept called "opportunity cost" that applies here. It means that whenever we say yes to something, we're automatically saying no to everything else at that time. If we attend a training seminar, we're not working at our desk. When we have lunch with one of our kids, we're not having lunch with anyone else.

The principle is simple: People who matter most in our lives must never be shortchanged by people at a different level.

A mother might feel her newly married daughter is disrespecting her because she doesn't spend as much time with her since the wedding. The daughter wants to invest in her new relationship but feels guilty when her mom feels slighted. She needs a well-crafted, realistic boundary and a well-crafted, respectful response: "Mom, I don't love you any less. But I'm married now, and that's the relationship I'm investing in the most. Our relationship is going to look a little different than before because it *is* different than before."

Once that boundary is in place, if the mom keeps pushing, the daughter simply needs to repeat it: "I'm sorry you feel that way. I don't love you any less. But the time I spend with you will look different."

Prepare

When conversations get tough, we reach into our toolboxes and grab whatever we're familiar with, then we wonder why the results aren't satisfying. If our communication tools have been mostly electronic, we might not have collected the right tools for the job. We know how to transmit words digitally but haven't had as much practice reading body language and facial expressions. We're missing the tools that help us sense the subtle reactions that happen during face-to-face conversations.

The time to collect the right tools and learn to use them well is before tough conversations happen. That's what we'll be doing in the rest of this book. The key to effective connection isn't talking more. Talking is easy; communicating is hard. The key is to find out what tools we're missing and obtain them.

Participate

Some of the most powerful tools we're missing in communication are listening tools. If we believe we're right, our ears don't work very well. If we listen at all, it's often just for the purpose of finding a way to change somebody else's mind.

We don't want to understand; we want to convince. We don't participate in the conversation; we try to run the conversation.

It's amazing how many people believe they're right. No matter what the topic, they have a perspective on it—and they assume it's correct. Logically, if I'm convinced that I'm right and you see things differently, then obviously you must be wrong.

I'm one of those people. And so are you.

We have views on just about everything. Over our lifetime, we've developed those views through our background, our language, our culture, our experience, our education. We look at an issue and feel like our perspective is crystal clear. After all, it's what we see, right?

If you have a perspective that's different from mine, I assume you're not seeing the situation clearly (since it's so obvious to me). So I figure that if I can convince you of the logic of my position, you'll instantly recognize where you're in error. I tell you why your perspective is wrong and mine is right. I feel like I'm providing a service to you so you can be right instead of wrong.

But after I explain my position, you don't go along with it. Since it's so clear to me, I assume you're just being stubborn. So I say it louder, thinking it will impact you more.

It doesn't work. The problem? We both believe our perspective is right and the other person's perspective is wrong. We're both talking, but our different perspectives keep us from seeing through each other's eyes. We're both trying to control the outcome of the conversation rather than being participants in it.

We can watch courtroom dramas to see how this works. Lawyers interrogate witnesses so the jury gets a more complete picture of the situation. If there are differing viewpoints, it could mean that someone is lying. But often it means that people saw the incident from different vantage points, and they each believe they're right because it's what they saw.

If every witness was telling the truth, wouldn't they all say the same thing? Probably not. Their perspective might be accurate but incomplete. The jury draws from those different perspectives to determine what really happened.

We often see this play out on social media. People have found a platform where they can say whatever they want. They disagree with someone (usually over politics or religion) and are convinced that their position is accurate. So they lay out their case, step by step, to prove they're right. They do it often and aggressively.

There are a whole lot of people doing just that, and all of them think their position is accurate. Who's right? Who's wrong? They're looking through different perspectives.

The same thing happens in relationships when the conversation turns tough. I think I'm right, and you think you're right. We're both convinced of our position and feel it's our duty to set the other straight. So we argue back and forth, trying to win the discussion.

Maybe there's a better way. We've been using our talking tools. Maybe we need to use our listening tools.

If we're both talking during a tough conversation, it pushes us apart. If we're both really listening to understand, it draws us together. That doesn't mean I need to give up and agree with you; it simply means I want to see from your vantage point. You have a different perspective, but it doesn't make sense to me when mine seems so obvious. So I need to set my position aside temporarily and see through your eyes. I need to participate with you instead of trying to take over the conversation.

In the courtroom scenario, I visit the crime scene and stand with you to see what you're seeing. Then you come across the street and look at the scene from my angle. We're not trying to see who's right and who's wrong; we're just trying to see the other person's perspective.

Practice

As relationships grow and develop, we need to keep using our best tools. Most of us feel like the communication tools we have are all we'll ever need. We got them as children and picked up others along the way. As adults, we've figured out ways to use those tools in our relationships—both the effective ones and the ineffective ones. It never occurs to us that we might need new tools and that it's possible to obtain them and learn to use them.

My wife bought a food processor last year. It was something she had considered for years but seemed like a luxury she could do without. After all, she had been chopping vegetables by hand for decades. That got the job done. It took a while, but she got the results she wanted.

Other people told her what a food processor could do. It sounded interesting, and she finally decided to give it a try. We opened the box, started reading the instructions, and assembled the unit. We grabbed a variety of veggies and decided it was time to experiment. She washed and peeled the carrots, and I cut the peppers into appropriate-sized chunks. I think we were both skeptical and definitely not enthusiastic as we turned the unit on and inserted the first carrot.

I'm not sure how long we stood there with our mouths open staring at the results. In less than a second, the carrot had been transformed into perfect slices.

For the next hour, we emptied the fridge as we tried different blades and tools. We studied the directions further to see what else we could do. Not only did the machine accomplish the tasks my wife had done by hand for years, but it also did it in a fraction of the time.

And it made nut butter, fresh nut butter made from a combination of nuts for a totally different flavor at a fraction of the grocery store cost. We had never been able to make nut butter because we didn't have the right tool.

She doesn't use the food processor every day like some people do. But we eat a lot of vegetables, and it has changed our perspective on food preparation. We lived without that tool for a really long time. Now that we've added it to our kitchen and practiced using it, the process of food preparation has become simpler and more efficient than ever. With the right tool, we can do things that were painfully slow, ineffective, or impossible in the past.

Sure, we've learned how to talk to each other. But communicating takes a more extensive set of tools than just talking. Better tools give us better options for growing our conversational skills.

Refreshing the Toolbox

Anyone, regardless of their age, can add new tools to their communication toolbox. The first step is to recognize which tools are missing. That can be done by seeing where the pain is in relationships that current tools won't handle. Then the search begins to find the tools that will do the job.

That means there's hope. If we have the right tools, we can become effective in communication. It doesn't mean every conversation will be perfect, because we're imperfect—and so are the people we communicate with. But with the right resources, we'll be able to approach those tough conversations with a clear, sensible perspective. We won't be intimidated by others because we won't see them as the enemy. We'll be able to focus on the issue while showing respect for the differing views of others.

When our toolbox contains only talking tools, tough conversations will always be challenging. Those tools have their place but need to be used well. If we misuse them, they become weapons. When we add listening tools, those tough conversations look different. Listening tools might take a while to get used to because they're unfamiliar, but they help us understand another person's point of view. Both kinds of tools can be abused, so we need to learn which tool works in different situations and with different temperaments.

A surgeon has a lot of tools at her disposal. Many of her tools utilize the most advanced technology. But she doesn't use them all every time she approaches the operating table. She uses the exact tool that's needed to perform a specific task.

At the same time, the quality of the tool by itself doesn't determine success; the skill of the surgeon is also important. The most skilled surgeon can't perform surgery with only her bare hands; she needs tools. Tools, by themselves, are useless unless a skilled surgeon picks them up. In the hands of an amateur, those same tools can be dangerous.

That's the key to navigating tough conversations. We can obtain the tools we need, but we also must learn to use them effectively. If we don't, we could cause a lot of pain in our relationships.

In the next few chapters, we'll explore the tools we need in our toolbox—the basic principles that make conversations work. Then we'll explore the skills needed to use those tools in the dynamic relationships we all experience, including those with spouses, kids, relatives, friends, work associates, and other people we encounter.

Finally, we'll learn a preventative approach. We'll learn how to build the foundation of a healthy relationship that allows us to have tough conversations when necessary. Healthy relationships don't just happen; they're crafted by normal people who have the right set of tools and the proper techniques. The good news? These tools and skills are available to everyone, not just experts. It takes time, intentionality, and practice, but effective communication is possible.

3

What People Need

Some people just need to change their Facebook status to "Needs Attention."

Anonymous

When I was growing up in Phoenix, most people had Bermuda grass lawns. Anywhere else, Bermuda grass would be considered a weed, and we'd fight to get rid of it. It takes very little water and grows in just about any type of soil. That makes it an ideal groundcover for the intense summer heat.

In the winter, Bermuda grass goes dormant. It turns completely dry and crunchy and brown. For all purposes, it looks dead. Once spring comes, all it takes is a little water and the lifeless turf begins to turn green.

Some people just accept the brown grass. But others want a green lawn year-round. There are two common solutions:

1. They can overseed the dormant lawn with rye grass, which grows well in the winter and dies off just as the Bermuda begins to come back.
2. They can paint their dormant lawn green.

Most homeowners choose the rye grass. But shopping centers and commercial buildings often choose the paint. When we lived there, it was always startling to visit a shopping center in the winter, step into what looked like a lush, green lawn—only to hear it crunch under our feet. Sometimes we would see the landscapers applying the paint with their tanks and sprayers, and the lawns would magically transform as they walked along.

There are two parts to a lawn: what's above ground (the part we see), and what's below ground (the part we don't see). What happens below ground determines what happens above ground. If we see wilted grass, we know the roots need more water. If the tips of the blades turn brown, it might mean they're getting too much water. If the grass looks dead, it might just be dormant. The key to a healthy lawn is to take care of what happens below ground.

That's true with people as well. What happens below the surface determines what people see in our lives. We want people to think highly of us, seeing us as people of high character and integrity. We want to be seen as people who really care.

There are two ways to do that:

1. We can do the things high-character, caring people do— hoping that people will think we actually have high character. (That's like painting the lawn.)

2. We can work on our character underground and in the dark, where nobody sees. We can become people of true character on the inside. Over time, that character will begin to grow and flourish on the outside.

People Watching

We can't fake character. If we're unhealthy on the inside, it'll begin to show on the outside over time. Plus, faking it is a lot of work. Real character is an inside job. If we develop it, people will see it on the outside.

Just as we study trees and plants to know if there's something wrong, we do the same with people. At first glance, they seem happy and it looks like everything's going well. We ask them how things are going, and they say, "Great. Couldn't be better."

But if we look in their eyes, we sense that something isn't right. Maybe the sparkle is missing, or we sense the slightest droop in their smile as we connect. It's subtle and easily overlooked in passing. If we're connecting through technology, it's even tougher to get those subtle cues.

If we take the time to be observant, we can sense whether someone's basic needs are being met. If those needs are unmet, we can tell by what's happening on the surface. If they are being met, we can see that as well.

We seek out relationships to meet our basic needs. For some reason, our most foundational needs can't be met in isolation. They're met through human connections.

Early in a relationship, those needs cause us to seek connection. Our needs are met, and we enjoy the relationship. Over time, the needs that were being met in the beginning start being ignored. Maybe we get busy, or distracted, or simply take the other person's needs for granted. We've gotten used to each other, and we don't work quite as hard at meeting those needs. But those needs are still real and present. It's like when the wife says, "You never tell me you love me anymore." The husband replies, "I told you when I married you. If it changes, I'll let you know."

The Six Basic Needs

When we observe unhealthy symptoms in others, what basic needs aren't being met?

There are probably as many theories about what people need as there are people. Here are a variety of approaches:

- Abraham Maslow presented his "Hierarchy of Human Needs,"[1] suggesting that basic needs must be met at the lowest levels (physiological, safety, love/belonging) or people won't be able to move to the highest levels (esteem, self-actualization).
- Manfred Max-Neef classified fundamental human needs as subsistence, protection, affection, understanding, participation, leisure, creation, identity, and freedom.[2]
- Anthony Robbins said that everyone's choices are based on trying to get their needs met in six areas: certainty, uncertainty, significance, connection/love, growth, and contribution. He suggested that all dysfunction comes out of an inability to have these needs met.[3]

We could probably build a case for all of these approaches, but we're talking here about relationships. Unmet needs in relationships cause problems, so we need to identify some of those areas that apply. Knowing what people need can explain why they often behave the way they do.

Based on my experience with people and relationships over the years, I've made my own list of the six needs that are present in just about every relationship. Different people have varying degrees of need in each area. The challenge comes when one person has a low level of need in the same area in which the other person in the relationship has a high level of need.

This isn't meant to be a comprehensive or final list. But it provides a place to start when we're exploring the basic communication challenges that take place between people.

Security

From birth, we have an innate need for safety and security. We want to know what we can count on so we have a secure anchor point for exploring the future. It's like standing on a crowded bus or train. When it stops suddenly, people instinctively grab for a railing to hang on to. They trust that it won't go anywhere.

Let's say I have a checking account and a savings account at my bank. Let's also say that my checking account is low. There's enough to pay the bills this month but nothing left over for frills or emergencies.

Then the refrigerator breaks. If I have ten dollars in my savings account, I'm going to be pretty stressed about the fridge. If I have one hundred thousand dollars in my savings account, I'm going to feel a lot better. My checking account balance hasn't changed, but having that reserve in savings, even if I'm not planning to use it, gives me a different perspective. There's a security beneath the surface that I can hang on to.

Relationships thrive on security. If we know our boss is committed to helping us grow in our career path, we're not as terrified when we make a major mistake. If we know our spouse is deeply committed to the relationship, we are free to have tough conversations without being intimidated or frightened of what will happen.

One person might have a low need for security, so they're excited about any possibility of change. If the other person has a high need for security, even a small change can be threatening. Put those two people into a relationship, and it can get pretty interesting.

The key is not to decide who's right and who's wrong. The key is to listen to the needs of the other person and try to understand their perspective. Only then can both people work creatively toward a solution that will meet both of their needs.

Adventure

Adventure sounds like the opposite of security, but it actually partners with it. Adventure has to do with leaving our comfort zones. If we spend a lot of time in our comfort zones, we become . . . well, comfortable. There's no incentive to explore outside the familiar.

Most growth happens when we move outside our comfort zones. That takes effort and risk. People with a high need for adventure can't wait to see what is out there that they've never experienced before. They're innately curious and want to move ahead. People with a low need for adventure tend to fear the unknown. Part of them wants to explore, but they want to do it in a safe environment.

Low adventure people want to watch the safari from the tour bus. High adventure people want to ride the cheetah. There's an obvious chance of conflict when we put those two people together. Both can get frustrated with the other because they're moving either too fast or too slow. It takes a deep level of communication to understand each other's position. When a person feels they've been genuinely listened to and heard, they trust the other person and are willing to choose a creative solution that works for both of them.

I know one couple who used to dread vacations together. Both wanted to relax, but one relaxed by being on the move the entire trip, while the other wanted to sit on the beach and read.

One wanted to go somewhere new every year, while the other wanted to revisit the familiar places to enjoy them again. They considered taking separate vacations but realized that would only put a deeper wedge between them. Instead, they worked together to create trips in which they could enjoy each other while finding creative ways to meet each other's needs.

One year, they saved for a river cruise in Europe. Each day there were stops in different cities where they could explore the culture and taste the cuisine for a few hours. When it was time for the ship to continue the journey, one spouse relaxed and read in the stateroom and watched the castles they were passing. The other went to the top deck to take part in organized activities. They were able to enjoy a world-class vacation that met each of their needs.

Growth

Growth is a natural part of being healthy, both physically and emotionally. But growth takes effort. When that effort feels overwhelming, some people decide it's not worth it.

We can try to ignore the natural instinct to grow, but growth takes place in spite of our efforts. Trying to stop growth is like trying to hold a beach ball underwater. We might be able to do it for a while, but it keeps popping up to the surface.

If people avoid the effort of growth, they often replace it by being distracted. They focus on something else like entertainment or busyness to keep them from feeling the need to grow. But under the surface, the need to grow is still there.

Someone said, "Busyness is the anesthetic for the pain of an empty life." If people ignore their basic need to grow, the result is often a life filled with activities, but inwardly they are disengaged and discouraged.

Relationships stagnate when they stop growing. They're like the Dead Sea—a body of water with no outlet in which the salt has built up to a point that no life can survive in it.

Acceptance

Deep inside, we want to know that we're not broken goods (even though we're all broken). We need to know that somebody thinks we're okay and they accept us as we are. We don't have to "clean up" for them. They know who we are, and they still value us.

Our early life experiences shape our views of ourselves. If the important people in our lives offered unconditional love, we felt valued. If we didn't experience that kind of love, we felt unaccepted and unworthy. Those early experiences follow us throughout our lives and influence the way we relate to others.

Years ago, the book *I'm OK, You're OK* quickly became a bestseller because people identified with the need for acceptance. When someone genuinely cares for us with no strings attached, we have the strength to handle the disappointments in life. Everybody needs someone who cares about them just the way they are, with no agenda.

Connection

Humans need other humans. Life was meant to be shared and finds its richest meaning in community.

When I'm traveling, something often moves me—a world-class sunset, an amazing meal, or just an experience that brings me joy. My first instinct is to think, "I wish Diane could see this." So I take a picture with my phone and send it to her so she can share the experience. More than once I've taken a picture of a meal I'm enjoying that makes me want to experience it with her by my side.

Roger was one of those independent people who said he didn't need anyone else. "I can take care of myself," he would say. "Relationships are just too much of a hassle." But deep inside, he knew it was an excuse. He was afraid to be vulnerable because he didn't want to be rejected.

Like Roger, many people don't want to do the hard work to learn interpersonal skills that lead to real connection. It's easier for them to say, "I don't need anybody" than to learn how to communicate effectively. Deep inside, it's an unmet need. If connection doesn't happen, it impacts the person's life in some very unhealthy ways.

Human moments have become more rare as they have been replaced by technological moments. When people communicate electronically without having face-to-face conversations, they miss the subtleties that draw people together. When we're physically present with someone and give them our undivided attention, we have a human moment. That's connection.

Purpose

We all need to know that we're not just taking up space on the planet. We're hardwired that way. We want to make a difference. We were created with a blend of temperament, passion, and interest that makes us unique. Nobody else is just like us, and nobody can contribute what we have to offer.

Too often, we compare ourselves to others. We see the contributions they're making, and ours feel insignificant by contrast. So we either give up trying (because we believe we don't have anything of value to give), or we try to copy others. We figure that if we do what they do, we'll at least be able to make some of the impact they make.

The problem is that when we try to imitate others, we rob the world of the unique contribution we were designed to make. Our uniqueness is the greatest tool we have to make a difference in society and in the lives of others.

That's especially true in relationships. If two people feel they have nothing to offer, they get caught in a meaningless cycle of activity. They're busy with many activities but nothing that leads them forward. Sometimes people are even attracted to each other through their lack of purpose, agreeing to a relationship in which they settle for each other. They start by working on projects side by side but end up on the couch fighting over the remote.

Two half people don't make one whole couple. Relationships can't be healthy if the people in those relationships are unhealthy.

Moving toward Maturity

When people can't meet their own basic needs, they are *dependent*. Somebody else has to meet their needs for them, or they won't survive. A brand-new baby is dependent, needing someone else to feed them, change them, and provide their basic needs. We don't mind, because it's expected of a baby.

There's an expectation, however, that people will eventually become *independent*. A newborn grows into a toddler, then a child, then a teenager, then an adult. During that process, they become more and more able to meet their own needs. When adults can't meet their own needs, we see them as outside the norm. Sometimes their inability stems from physical or developmental issues that create dependency. At other times, people just simply have not made the transition to independence because they've gotten used to letting other people take care of their needs.

Our kids are in their thirties, and they're independent. We're still emotionally involved with them and connect with them as often as possible. But they have their own lives and make their own choices. We're connected—if we were out of the picture, it would be painful for them but they would be okay.

Independent people are those whose basic needs have been met, providing the foundation for healthy relationships. Dependent people look to others to meet their needs instead of taking responsibility for them. Most relationship issues result from dependent people trying to get others to meet their needs. When it doesn't happen, it puts a strain on the relationship.

When conversations get tough, dependent people often blame each other for the problem. A better way is to enter those conversations with a healthy, independent perspective and to bring resources together to work on the issue. Healthy people focus on fixing the problem, not trying to fix the other person.

Children grow into adults. But if their needs aren't met along the way, they become adults who still function as children. That's where relationships get messed up and communication gets challenging.

It's time to grow up.

Tools for Healthy Conversations

I read an article a while back that discussed a long-standing stereotype about women—that they are not as good at fixing things as men. The article suggested that there may have been some truth to that perspective in the past, but there was an unexpected reason: they'd been given cheap tools.

Manufacturers marketed the best-quality tools to men, assuming that women didn't need good tools if they didn't have the skills. But the article suggested that because they had inferior tools, women were limited in what they could do. Give them the right tools, and their skill level would increase.

That's an interesting premise and leads to a valid point: If we don't have the right tools, we won't be able to get the best results.

The same is true in communication. To build world-class conversations, we need the best possible tools. We've picked up tools throughout our lives that we use when we communicate with others. Some of those tools are effective, while others need to be replaced. Sometimes we're limited in what we can do because the exact tool we need is missing from our toolbox.

The key to handling tough conversations is to have the tools we need for construction, maintenance, and repair. In this section, we'll explore six tools that are essential for the best results:

1. perspective
2. trust
3. ownership
4. emotions
5. time
6. respect

If the tools are missing, we can obtain them. If they're inferior, we can replace them. It doesn't matter if we're building, repairing, or maintaining our relationships; we can't engage in effective conversations if we don't have the right tools.

What's in your toolbox?

4

Tool #1—You Gotta Learn to Dance (Perspective)

> Anyone who answers without listening is foolish and confused.
>
> Proverbs 18:13 EXB

My wife was walking through our neighborhood and met a woman who had just moved in a few doors down. They were standing in her driveway swapping stories and getting acquainted. It was a chance to help the new neighbor feel welcome.

As they were talking, another neighbor who lived next door on a higher lot walked out to the fence and started yelling. "Your tree is too tall," he said. "It's blocking my view. Don't you know we have rules about that around here? I'm going to report you to the association." He continued his venomous attack until his wife came out and pulled him back inside.

I'm sure our new neighbor was thinking, *What in the world have we gotten into?* A couple of weeks later, they had the tree removed. I'm guessing she had some long discussions with her husband about the incident, and they probably weren't very positive. They had been attacked and naturally formed an opinion about their neighbor.

I've had occasional conversations with this man in the past. He's always seemed a little eccentric but never vicious. But a few months ago, he met me in my driveway. He said, "I've seen you leading a seminar a few times in your driveway about three o'clock in the morning, playing music from the back of your car. You had chairs set up, and the noise woke me up. So I got up to see what was going on and saw the lights on at your place. I was just wondering what that was all about."

I've never led a seminar in my driveway at three o'clock in the morning. I don't know that I've ever seen three o'clock in the morning.

That was my first clue that something was wrong. We learned that he's experiencing dementia that appeared rather suddenly. He's become much more forceful, and we've seen other family members around the house to take care of him.

Our new neighbors didn't have that perspective. It would have been natural for them to begin a negative relationship, seeing this elderly man as the enemy. But a new perspective changes the way we experience things.

Someone said, "In the absence of data, we tend to make things up." That's why it's important to keep talking about hard issues. If we don't, we won't know what the other person is thinking. So we start believing our made-up perspectives, imagining things that aren't there and assuming they're true.

When people have an issue with someone else, they are often uncomfortable talking to them about it. So they take the easier path, which is to talk with everyone else instead of that person.

Any time we talk *about* people without talking *to* them, we run the risk of damaging our relationship with them. The only way to build healthy relationships is to go directly to the person involved, even if it's challenging.

Haters in the Shadows

Authors discover this quickly. People read their books, form opinions, and write them in book reviews, blog posts, or other publications. If they disagree with the author, they often write scathing reviews about the book. But they often critique the author's character as well.

I've always found it interesting that these critics present their opinions so strongly and confidently, but they've never had a conversation with the author. They speak from the shadows, saying things they might never say face-to-face.

Years ago, after my first book was published, I read a review a college professor published in his school's alumni journal. He said that while the book was one of the best books on the subject he had ever read, he was concerned that I had quoted people he considered to be the most damaging to what he believed and taught. It was guilt by association. Since I quoted them, he assumed I agreed with their entire position and was siding with the enemy. As a result, he couldn't recommend the book.

When I read that, I was more disappointed than angry. He was entitled to disagree with me, but he told others that I held a position I didn't. I believe that even people I disagree with say some really intelligent things occasionally, and I'm comfortable quoting them. Evidently, he didn't share that opinion, and he used that as the basis of his critique. He wasn't attacking just my content; he was attacking my character.

If he and I had sat down over coffee, we could have talked about it. He could have said, "Here's my concern about what you wrote, and here's what I'm planning to say about it. But I'd really like to hear your perspective before I do that."

If that had happened, I might actually be okay with a negative review from him. If he had showed me enough respect to connect first, he wouldn't be speaking from the shadows.

Dancing Alone

When a conversation gets tough, many people simply disappear. They don't like conflict, so they disengage from the other person to avoid confrontation. But at the same time, they put their feelings in writing where they can be aggressive without having to deal with the other person's response. They might also start talking to others about what the person is doing.

Communication is kind of like being on a dance floor with a partner, and we're trying to dance together. Dancing isn't an exact science, and success depends on being attentive and responsive to what the other person is doing. We can't ignore each other.

When we criticize someone behind their back, it's like ignoring our partner on the dance floor. Instead of trying to work with them, we simply criticize every move they make. We yell about their lack of skill and how inferior they are to us. We're dancing alone instead of dancing together.

A good friend of mine owns a contracting business. It can be a cutthroat field in which lawsuits are often assumed even before a project begins. Most communication takes place through email. He told me that those email conversations often escalate quickly, and each reply becomes more heated and vicious than the last. In a matter of a few hours, tempers flare and accusations are made. "It just becomes the way people communicate," he said. "It's all being done in writing, and it's easier for people to yell when they're not sitting across the table from each other."

He said that when the first email comes through that hints at rising emotion, he doesn't reply. He simply picks up the phone and says, "Hey, I got your email. What's going on? Let's talk about it." Sometimes he'll take the time to drive across town to have lunch with someone just so they can look each other in the eyes and share their perspectives. "It doesn't matter how tough they are or how heated they sound in writing," he says. "Almost everybody softens when you sit down with them."

That's a key principle: We can't text a tough conversation. The tougher a situation gets, the more we need to move toward face-to-face connection and attempt to see the other person's perspective.

Different Views

So how can people who are so different work together when conversations get tough? We need to look through the other person's eyes and see what they see—not so we can agree with them but so we can understand them.

My wife and I saw a sculpture in front of an office complex that demonstrates the concept well. We stood on opposite sides of it, knowing that we were looking at the same sculpture. From her side, it was obviously a slim, attractive girl wrapped in a delicate gown. But from my side, it was a huge nose with a giant nostril at the bottom.

We could describe what we saw and think the other person was completely crazy. She could wonder why I was chuckling at the absurdity of the statue, while I could wonder how she could think it was beautiful. We could argue all day about what we saw because it was so obvious to us. Then we could drive home in silence, feeling like the other person was just being stubborn.

What could we do differently? I could walk to her side and see what she was seeing. Then we could walk over to my side and see what I was seeing. Then we could hold hands and explore the statue together because we had seen each other's point of view.

Fear of Footwork

When two people dance together, they have a common goal. They want to have a pleasant experience and enjoy each other's company. When it works, it's magic. Things can happen on the dance floor that never happen when we're alone or standing still.

Before my daughter's wedding, my wife and I took a few ballroom dance lessons. I knew there would be the obligatory father-daughter dance, and I didn't want to be embarrassed. But it was more than that. I wasn't concerned about only myself and how people saw me. I was also concerned about my relationship with my daughter. Next to my wife, she's the most important girl in my entire world. It was her special day, and I wanted to give her the focus she deserved. I wanted to dance well for her, not for me. I don't know that I succeeded technically, and she probably had some bruises to show for the experience. But sharing that dance with her was one of the highlights of my life. My relationship with her was important enough to put in the work.

Dancing isn't a scripted exercise. There are patterns that have to be learned, but a couple improvises based on what they're feeling individually. They don't know exactly what the other person will do and how they'll respond to each other's moves. It can be messy for a while, and people step on each other's toes. Nobody is in control, and that can feel uncomfortable.

That's how it is with conversations. When they get tough, we can get frustrated when the other person doesn't respond the way we expect. Conversations can be messy and really uncomfortable. But to keep our conversations healthy, we need to remember one thing: we gotta keep dancing.

Dance Lessons

How do we learn to dance together? We take lessons. We work on the basic patterns and then learn how to use them to improve. We get better and try new things. We learn how to anticipate the unexpected from our partner and how to respond appropriately.

Learning to dance is a lot like learning to communicate effectively:

- It takes energy.
- It takes practice.
- There has to be give-and-take and cooperation (one person moves their foot forward while the other person moves theirs backward).
- It involves emotion (which is why dancing always takes place to music).
- There is variety (slow dances, energetic dances, exciting dances).
- The rules provide the structure that makes it enjoyable.
- There are turns that can make us dizzy unless we stay focused.
- There are "dips" that require one person to trust another.

"But they're being unreasonable," you say. "They're the problem. They need to change, or we'll never figure this out!"

That might be true in both dancing and communication. If we both feel the other person needs to change before anything can happen, we're at an impasse. There are always two perspectives, which is what provides the potential for great solutions. It takes humility to admit that we might need to change as well.

It's easy to focus on the other person's clumsiness. But if we want rich conversation, we have to put in the work to master the steps. Maybe one person learns quicker than the other and gets frustrated. They get their toes stepped on. Instead of quitting, they keep practicing until they learn to sense the other person's moves. Little by little, they find success.

We know the value of vibrant communication, and we work toward it. But when challenging issues arise, it's easy to stomp on each other's feet. Our energy goes toward attacking each other instead of toward resolving the issue. No matter how tough the conversation becomes, we need to constantly remind ourselves—and each other—of the most important perspective: if a relationship has value, it's worth the effort.

We might have to say, "I'm so frustrated with you right now that I can hardly see straight. But I'm not giving up, and I'm not going away. You're worth it. We're worth it." We might have to walk off the dance floor so we can calm down. But the separation is temporary and always includes the commitment to come back and keep dancing.

Dance Practice

This dance takes place every time we interact with another person. The give-and-take of negotiating a business transaction, dealing with a client's objections, or interacting with a friend at church means we're dancing every day. We have plenty of chances to practice in our casual relationships, preparing us for connection in those relationships that matter most to us.

Think about sitting with a salesperson in a car showroom trying to get the best price on a vehicle. They might be outgoing and friendly or quiet and seemingly sincere. If you've had bad experiences with car salespeople in the past, you'll be watching their dance moves to see if you can trust them. What they say determines what you say, which determines how they respond, which determines your next action. It's like dancing with a stranger, trying to figure out what they're going to do next. Instead of seeing them as the enemy who has to be beaten, you focus on the issue at hand: getting the car you want in a way that provides an honest outcome for both you and the salesperson.

This morning I saw a mini-dance as I waited to board a cross-country flight. A passenger stood in line as the gate agent checked people in. Suddenly, he recognized her as someone from his past and approached her with a hug. "How are you? Wow! It's been so long since I've seen you. How have you been?"

"Good," she said. "Really good. How about you?"

"Good. Really, really good."

"That's good," she said. "Is your family good?"

"Yeah, they're really good," he said. "How about your kids?"

"Oh, yeah, they're good. They're all good."

"Good, good. Really good," he responded.

It was funny to watch, because they were trying to dance. They tried to connect, but they were taking baby steps. Neither was sure what to say, so they said everything was good. Eventually, he boarded the plane as their awkward conversation ended, and she went back to her duties at the gate. (She was probably still wondering who he was.)

I don't fault them, because we all find ourselves in that situation. Sometimes we don't know what to say, so we just exchange a few "goods" and move on when the conversation gets uncomfortable. But if a relationship is one that two people value, they keep dancing. They keep exploring their common ground and their perspectives to find ways to connect more fully.

Value motivates us to continue the dance. Focusing on the value of our relationships gives us the reason to stay committed to the dance when things get tough.

Practical Steps for Gaining Perspective

So we've decided to stay in the dance. What can we do to build those rhythms and smooth out the footwork to facilitate healthy conversations? Here are some practical steps:

- *Commit to face-to-face connection.* As uncomfortable as tough conversations might be, they need to happen eyeball to eyeball. That doesn't mean we can never talk on the phone, use video calling, text, or email each other. But those are supplements to in-person conversations, not replacements. Face-to-face conversation provides a better opportunity to see the perspective of the other person accurately.

- *Get used to being uncomfortable.* Comfort is great, but it can't come at the expense of a relationship. When things get uncomfortable, it's because we're not looking at both perspectives. Discomfort should be a signal to face the problem, not a trigger to withdraw or escape.

- *Don't try to fix others.* There are no guarantees that other people will change. It would be nice, but it's not realistic. The only person we have control of in any relationship is ourselves. That's where we need to put our energy. Until we've worked on ourselves, it's futile to work on anyone else. We need to look inside before blaming outside.

- *Keep building momentum.* Just as it takes time and practice to become proficient as a dancer, it takes time and practice to communicate effectively with others. Conversation is a dynamic exercise because we can't predict how it will turn out. We don't know the other person's perspective until we explore beyond our own. It's good to use our conversational "dance steps" when we're in conflict, but it's even better to practice them before the conflict—when things are going well and we feel connected. It's awkward to have a tough conversation with a cranky co-worker if we haven't had a few casual conversations with them along the way.

- *Look for common ground.* Someone said, "If two people see things exactly the same way, one of them is unnecessary." People are going to disagree because they have different perspectives. Focusing on the differences drives us apart, but looking for the things we can agree on draws us together.

- *Fight for the relationship.* Too many people give up in tough conversations when they get tired of trying. But if the relationship has value, it's worth fighting for. The worst dancing is better than hours of playing solitaire.

5

Tool #2—Confidence in Communication (Trust)

A relationship without trust is like a cell phone
without service. And what do you do with a cell
phone with no service? You play games.

Unknown

When I was growing up, I used to hop on my bike about
9:00 in the morning and take off. I never had a destination; I just wanted to explore. My mom would say, "Where
are you going?" "I don't know," I'd reply. "Well, be home in
time for lunch."

For the next three or four hours, I would ride. Sometimes I'd
ride alone. Sometimes I'd find friends to ride with, and we'd
ride east to Scottsdale or west to Glendale. We'd go through
residential areas, take shortcuts through the desert, or find canal

banks to use as mini-freeways. I never worried about anything happening, and my mom evidently trusted that I'd be okay.

Things are a lot different today. When my kids were little, I'd say, "Okay, make sure you don't go past that driveway down there and make sure you can always see me." Then I'd stand outside to watch. I trusted them but not those they might encounter around the corner who could harm them.

What changed? Why were my parents so trusting and I wasn't?

I think the change happened over a few decades as we saw more and more news stories about people hurting kids. There probably weren't any more incidents than there had been in the past, but the media made them more visible. So it felt like it was happening more often. Little by little, parents became fearful and kept their kids closer to home.

We used to live in a trusting culture punctuated by occasional episodes of harm. Now we live in an untrusting culture punctuated by occasional episodes of integrity.

If news stations showed stories that accurately reflected the percentage of good and bad events that happened, nobody would watch. When there's a plane crash, people are glued to their televisions. But nobody would watch a story about the tens of thousands of commercial flights every day that are uneventful.

Horrible news stories make us feel as if the world is unsafe and no one can be trusted. That mistrust impacts all our relationships as we begin to view those relationships through a low-trust lens. We're suspicious of people instead of trusting.

The result? People install hidden cameras in their homes to catch misbehaving babysitters, set up alarms to deter burglars, and pay for protection against identity theft. We assume that salespeople are more concerned about their own finances than ours, that lawyers are all unsavory, that politicians have impure motives.

Maybe that's why trust takes so long to build but is so easy to destroy. We assume other people aren't trustworthy until they prove otherwise. Our default setting has become "mistrust" instead of "trust." That can really mess with the way we communicate.

Every parent faces that day when they leave a young teen home alone for the first time. It's terrifying because they have to trust them. If the experience goes well, the parent will find it a little easier to trust the next time. But if the teen violates the rules, the situation can lead to a tough conversation. The more trust there is in the relationship, the smoother that conversation will go. The less trust there is, the harder it will be to communicate. The best way to create a smooth road for conversation is to build trust into a relationship.

How We Trust

Most people find themselves somewhere along a trust continuum. At one end, we trust everyone. At the other end, we trust no one. Our life experiences have probably determined where we land.

Trust No One	Trust Everyone

Maybe we started with high trust, but someone violated our trust along the way. At that point, we moved to the left on the continuum. It's also possible that we started with low trust, but someone believed in us and related to us with integrity—and we moved to the right on the continuum.

Where Does Trust Come From?

A good friend of ours got married last year. She invited us over for dinner so we could meet her future husband a few months before the wedding. We had heard great things from her about him, so we assumed he was a great guy. He was (and is), but our first impression was hard to shake. This guy could have been a long-lost identical twin brother of our family doctor. He looked like him, talked like him, had the same gestures, and wore his hair the same way. Fortunately, we like our doctor and trust him. If we didn't, we probably would have had trouble liking and trusting someone who looks just like him. That's because, in a sense, we "profile" people. If they remind us of someone we know, it's hard not to think of them in the same way—whether good or bad.

Whenever we encounter someone for the first time, our trust in them is neutral. We don't trust or distrust them. But we immediately size them up to decide if they're trustworthy. If they remind us of someone we trust, we might feel slightly trusting toward them. If they remind us of someone we distrust, we might feel slight mistrust toward them.

Before they ever say a word, we profile them. That gives us a filter for our first conversation with them. If we have a slight mistrust, we'll listen for words to reinforce that feeling. But our first encounter could change our minds and develop trust. If we feel slightly trusting, we'll assume their words will fit that assumption. But they could say something that immediately lowers that trust.

Over time, our trust in them goes up or down based on their actions and words. This doesn't happen all at once; trust is built layer by layer. If our exposure to that person over time is consistently positive, we tend to see them as trustworthy. That's when we start to relax. We don't analyze what's happening each time we're together. We've moved them into the trusted category and finally allow ourselves to enjoy the relationship. We like the other person. We look forward to our encounters with them. We feel safe with them.

That's the way close relationships begin, and that's what they're supposed to look like. So why don't they stay that way? How does trust disappear?

How We Lose Trust

Sometimes a person we trust completely violates that trust in an instant, such as when we catch them in a lie or we discover they are living a secret life. We're shocked and feel like we've been blindsided. We trusted them, and now we don't. We believed in them, and now we're hurt. Why? Because they're not safe anymore. We allowed ourselves to relax, and we got hurt. Now our guard is up.

But most of the time, a loss of trust happens slowly. We notice something in their speech, in their tone of voice, or in the look in their eyes that feels inconsistent. It's just under the surface, but we dismiss it because we trust them. We tell ourselves that we just misread the situation. After all, they're trustworthy, and we've learned to relax with them. We believe in them, so it's just a tiny blip on the radar. We tell ourselves that it's just our imagination.

If those blips continue to show up, they catch our attention. Maybe we ask the other person about something, and they deny it—or tell us we just don't understand. They might even say, "What? Don't you trust me?" Their reaction causes us to feel guilty, and we back off. But the damage has been done.

"So what do I do when there's no trust in a relationship, and the other person hasn't given me any reason to trust them? Is there hope?"

Earlier in this book, we found that we can't pin our hopes on another person changing. It's possible for people to change, but if we depend on it for our happiness, we'll likely be frustrated. The only person we can change is ourselves. So if the other person in the relationship can't be trusted, it's up to us to determine the boundaries to keep communication from becoming toxic. Instead of focusing on their lack of trustworthiness, we can focus on the one thing we can actually do something about: we can become trustworthy ourselves.

The Importance of Senses to Building Trust

The most important senses we use in communication are sight, sound, and touch (which is why electronic communication puts us at such a disadvantage). The less input we get from those senses, the less we have to work with—and the harder it is to build trust.

PHYSICAL PRESENCE

When we're with another person, we hear more than their words; we pick up their tone of voice and the subtle inflections that help us tune in to their true motives. We also use our vision to provide clues to their meaning or intentions. Some of those clues are so slight that they register below the level of consciousness, such as a slight loss of eye contact or a tiny nervous gesture. But they still register.

For example, we're having a tough conversation with someone and wonder whether they're telling the truth. Certain involuntary signals often reveal that people are lying:

- Their gestures become stiffer than normal as they try to control their reactions.
- They casually touch their nose or throat.
- They smile with only their mouth instead of their whole face.
- They delay their response, such as saying thank you for a gift but smiling a few seconds later.
- They stare at us and stop blinking in a subconscious effort to appear in control.

Just because someone demonstrates one of these responses doesn't mean they're lying. But a combination of them (or actions that are different than usual) might cause us to question their motives.

We also use our vision to observe a host of things that provide context. We notice if eye contact is strong or broken; we see the slight movements of their lips that hint at the truth; we observe the furrowed brow, the body language, and the gestures that let us peek inside their motives. We might not consciously notice such things, but our brains instinctively process that data.

VERBAL PRESENCE

When we communicate on the phone, we hear tone of voice. But while many signals take place verbally, it's harder to judge the meaning of those signals without the visual. When there's an uncomfortable pause during a conversation, it's tough to evaluate the meaning behind the silence when we can't see the other person.

If people are trying to avoid telling the truth, they often provide subtle verbal cues:

- They repeat our words: "No, I did not leave the door unlocked."
- They stop using contractions: "I did not do that" instead of "I didn't do that."
- They provide too much information, trying to appear open.
- If we change the subject, they go along with us willingly to escape the accusation. (If they're telling the truth, they don't want to change the subject until they clarify the issue.)
- They talk faster or more than usual.
- They add phrases such as, "To be truthful . . ." or "I swear on a stack of Bibles . . ."

Again, a single cue doesn't mean they're lying. But when there are several, red flags go up in our minds.

That's why it's so hard to have challenging conversations without being face-to-face; we miss those subtle cues. I've often had conversations with people through video messaging when it's available and appropriate. It's still not perfect, but it's better than words alone. At least we can see facial expressions, even if we miss those tiny cues that can be sensed only in person.

Written Presence

It's great to hear from someone in writing. When I see an email from a good friend in my in-box, it's the first one I open. I can't wait to see what they have to say.

But when I read their words, I have to picture them saying those words. I insert their tone of voice, facial expressions, and body language. Based on my relationship with them, I make assumptions about what they're thinking. That's dangerous. I don't know what they're thinking because they might not have chosen words that adequately express their feelings. I may jump to conclusions that are inaccurate, but I believe them to be true.

Written words alone are always the last resort when seeking impactful, honest communication.

Together for Trust

Nothing substitutes for physical presence. Trust is built when we're together.

When I'm traveling, I don't have physical presence with my wife. So I make sure I call home every night to hear her voice, and we usually text back and forth several times during the day. It's not ideal, but it's intentional. We work hard at staying connected when we're apart.

Sometimes we are in situations where we have to be separated from people for months at a time and physical presence is impossible. When that happens, we need to keep connected through as many senses as possible.

- When physical presence isn't possible, we switch to video phone calls (so we can hear and see the other person).
- When video calls aren't possible, we switch to regular phone calls (so we can at least hear their voice).
- When phone calls aren't possible, we switch to connecting in writing (texting, email, etc.). But the frequency should be increased to maintain the relationship. If all I could do was text for a few days, I would send quick, fun messages multiple times during the day so the other person knows I'm thinking of them. It's not ideal, but it lets them know I'm focused on them and being intentional about the relationship.

Technology should be a way of enhancing our communication, not replacing it.

Practical Steps for Building Trust

Warren Buffet said, "It takes twenty years to build a reputation and five minutes to ruin it."[1] When trust is violated, we can't just say, "I'm sorry" and assume that trust has been fully restored. Apologizing is important and allows the relationship to move forward. But it takes repeated action to demonstrate that we're trustworthy again. Words have to be backed up with consistency.

Here are some practical strategies for building the trust that provides a solid foundation for tough conversations:

- *Keep promises.* Sometimes we assume that people will forget about the promises we've made. It's convenient to think that way but unrealistic. They won't forget, and failure to carry through on our promises puts us in the nontrustworthy column. If we hit a snag and know we can't deliver, we need to be proactive and let them know immediately. They might be counting on us, so we need to handle our promises with integrity.

- *Admit mistakes.* When politicians are caught in unethical behavior, they almost always apologize. But somehow, it feels hollow. We wonder if they're sorry for their behavior or sorry they got caught. Trust is built when we admit mistakes before others know they happened. Most people can forgive a mistake when they're told about it early rather than having to find out after the fact.

- *Listen.* Nothing builds trust like genuine listening. Looking someone in the eyes and letting them talk without interrupting are rare gifts. We need to listen simply for understanding, not so we can reply to what's been said. When listening is genuine, it cements people together more quickly than just about any other technique.

- *Be loyal to others when they're not around.* If we talk badly about someone when they're absent, the person who hears us assumes we'll talk badly about them when they're not around. If we develop a reputation for speaking only encouraging truth about others, others will trust our words.

- *Trust people with our feelings.* When we let others into areas of our hearts that aren't normally exposed, they know we've trusted them with that information. This opens the door for them to do the same, and trust between us grows.

- *Check in with others.* If we sense there's a barrier between us and someone else, we have to have the courage to ask, "Are we good? Is there anything between us that we're not talking about? Are you holding something back that I need to hear?" Then we need to listen without defensiveness.

- *Hear both sides.* Proverbs 18:13 says, "Anyone who answers without listening is foolish and confused" (EXB). We don't have to agree with someone to show them respect; we just need to listen and value their perspective. That puts the focus on fixing the issue rather than attacking the relationship.

- *Be on time.* This might seem insignificant, but it's another form of keeping a promise. When people know they can count on us to show up when we say we will, they gain trust in our consistency. Being late says, "What I'm doing is more important than what you're doing."

- *Care.* We need to genuinely explore the lives of others with no motive other than to get to know them. Doing so tells them we value them just for who they are. When people experience unconditional acceptance, they have the freedom to make mistakes and be human—something that is only safe to do around people they trust.

- *Be predictable.* This doesn't mean we can't be creative. It means our behaviors are consistent. Predictability becomes invisible over time because it's simply what people expect from us. When we do mess up, it will stand out because it's such a contrast to what they've come to expect. That's a good thing. Surprises are okay, but consistency builds trust.

- *Face tough stuff together.* Trust isn't built by being the lone ranger. When tough times come, we need to work as a team to get through them together. Independence is valuable, but interdependence strengthens both people.

When trust is high in a relationship, everything works better. When trust is low, everything gets complicated. That's why trust is one of the vital ingredients for effective communication and impactful conversation.

6

Tool #3—Staying on Your Side of the Checkerboard (Ownership)

> You cannot change the circumstances, the seasons,
> or the wind, but you can change yourself.
>
> Jim Rohn[1]

Savings Accounts Are Dead."

That was the headline of an article in this morning's newspaper. It seems that most banks are offering checking accounts that provide better interest rates than their savings accounts. But people are reluctant to switch their funds, because they've had those savings accounts for years. They're comfortable. They're familiar.

We opened our basic checking account and a savings account when we moved to California in 1990. It's what everybody did back then, so we did the same thing. The idea was that you needed a checking account as a place to hold money that you were spending, and you needed a savings account to start earning for the future. All you had to do was leave that money in savings, and it would grow over time.

A few years later, we were talking to someone at our bank as he looked at our accounts on a screen. "You know," he said, "we should move you into this special kind of checking account. It actually pays you interest, and there is no fee." That sounded logical, so we did it.

We still have that checking account. The average interest we earn is about two cents per month. That means that over the years, I doubt we've earned enough to buy a venti mocha at Starbucks. I might be able to afford a shot of vanilla syrup and add the mocha later.

The other day, my wife said, "Maybe we should close down my savings account and put the money somewhere else." I don't remember what I said in response, but the little voice in my head said, "No! You can't get rid of a savings account! What about the future?"

Old perspectives are hard to change. What worked years ago might not be appropriate anymore. But because those things are familiar, we're reluctant to do anything different.

Time for a Change

That can be true in relationships as well. The communication patterns we used early in a relationship may have worked in the past but have become ineffective in the present.

I recently went to the ninetieth birthday party of a man I had worked with back in the 1970s. It was a great event, and I was able to connect with good friends whom I hadn't seen since that time.

Because we hadn't seen each other for decades, we started talking about things from the past, even using the same conversation styles we had used before. But the more we talked, the more different the conversations became. We were different people than we were all those years ago, and had to reconnect as the people we were now—not the people we used to be. The more we talked, the richer our conversations became.

In biblical times, people used wineskins to hold new wine. That new wine would ferment inside the wineskin over time, and the skin was flexible enough to handle the expansion. It was an appropriate way to store newly made wine.

Over time, the wineskin would lose its elasticity and become brittle. It was still good for storing old wine, but if new wine was put in it, the skin would tear from the expansion and fermentation. The wine would be lost. New wine needed new wineskins.

In the early stages of any relationship, communication is fairly simple. The interaction is basic and safe and expands as the relationship matures. We learn patterns of conversation that work well, and they meet our needs for a long time.

Over time, relationships often stop growing. They become stagnant. The wineskins (communication patterns) still work because nothing is changing. But when the dynamics of a relationship start to change and new things happen, those old patterns won't last very long. When relationships grow, communication needs to grow.

If old communication styles get in the way of that growth, it's easy to blame the other person. "You never listen," or "You only think about yourself," or "You'll never change, so this relationship is hopeless" become common perspectives. We feel like giving up, because the other person isn't cooperating. We become a victim of their choices, and our happiness and security are based on what they do or say.

We feel helpless. If the other person doesn't change or cooperate, what are we supposed to do?

The People Whisperer

The Horse Whisperer was a late '90s movie in which Robert Redford calmly and patiently won the trust of a traumatized horse and turned it into a strong but compliant animal. He started by simply sitting nearby and watching it for days at a time, connecting quietly until he built trust.

I remember thinking, "How could someone simply sit and stare at a horse for hours at a time?" My wife suggested that it was the same reason she could sit through a movie and stare at Robert Redford for hours at a time.

But something deeper was happening. Redford's character had no guarantees about whether or not he could tame that horse. But he knew that nothing would happen if he tried to force change. He didn't become upset when the horse didn't cooperate. He didn't yell or berate the horse for its behavior. He didn't let his emotions be dictated by what the horse did or didn't do.

He knew there was only one thing he could control: himself. That kept him from being a victim of the horse's behavior. He simply sat in the horse's presence and allowed the horse to be what he was. He didn't use force; he used influence. Just being there and accepting the horse built trust over time, and eventually the horse began to respond to him.

Obviously, people are not horses. Our job isn't to make people comply with our wishes. We want to find a way for two different people with two different perspectives to be in one healthy relationship.

There's a principle here. When we try to force people to change or behave in a certain way, we're setting ourselves up for frustration. We can influence them by coming alongside them and simply being in their lives, watching and studying and accepting them. But there's no guarantee they'll change.

It's critical that we don't become a victim of their choices. We're responsible for ourselves, not for them. If our happiness and identity are based on what another person does, we've given them power over our lives. We need to take ownership for ourselves, not give it away to someone else.

It's like playing checkers. We move our checkers across the board, and the other person moves theirs. Our job is to control our move and then to respond when the other person makes a move. We can't control how the other person plays; we can only control how we respond. It would be inappropriate to run around the table and take over for them if they're not playing the way we think they should.

During tough conversations, we get frustrated when the other person doesn't respond the way we want them to. Maybe we find ourselves feeling angry at their words. At that point, we can choose to give in to our anger, or we can make the choice to handle the anger appropriately. If we give in, we're no longer in control. We're letting their choices determine how we feel.

Effective communication can take place only when we stay on our side of the checkerboard. We can't control what another person does or says, even if we're frustrated with how they interact with us. We can only control the moves we make and how we respond to their moves.

It's kind of like teaching someone how to do something but getting frustrated when they don't learn quickly enough. We want to jump in and do it for them because it seems easier than watching them struggle and seemingly waste time.

When my wife got a computer for her business, she signed up for a year's worth of one-on-one instruction. She could go back to the store once a week and an instructor would walk her through a new skill.

Some of the instructors would explain a process, demonstrate it, and then let her do it a few times until it became familiar. Other instructors would explain and demonstrate, assuming that it made sense to her. But she would have to say, "No, I need to try it myself to get it." She could sense their frustration as she tried tasks herself.

Committed to Insanity

The popular definition of insanity is, "Doing the same thing over and over and expecting different results." That's such a simple concept that we often overlook its impact, especially in relationships. We've learned patterns of communication over time by seeing what works and what doesn't. We've discovered how to push another person's buttons, and they've figured out how to push ours.

We decide to work on a relationship because we want it to grow. But when we hit tough conversations, we fall back on our old patterns. Instead of making conscious choices about how to respond, we put our brain on autopilot. We say something without thinking, and we let the other person push those old buttons that determine our responses. We forget that we can choose how we respond. We don't have to be a victim of our emotions; we have the power to choose.

Assuming those old patterns will work in a new situation is insanity. If we want different outcomes, we need to make different choices. Our ineffective perspectives are getting in the way of effective ones. The old wineskins are brittle and need to be replaced.

What do we replace them with? Here are a few perspectives to consider if we want to make our conversations more effective.

We replace blaming others with taking ownership. We need to take responsibility for what we do in any relationship or conversation. When we assume the other person is the problem, we short-circuit the communication process. Blaming others is unproductive because we give up control of ourselves in the relationship. When we suggest that they need to change in order for anything to be different, we put them in charge of the relationship and we give up our influence.

We replace expectations with expectancy. When we have expectations of what needs to happen, we'll usually be disappointed. We play out conversations ahead of time, thinking of what we need to say, how they'll respond, and what we'll say when they do. But people almost never read the script we've written for them, and we get frustrated. They don't meet our expectations, and we don't know how to respond.

It's better to have expectancy. We don't know how things will turn out but simply anticipate the results. We make choices about what we say and how we respond during the conversation, but we don't plan them ahead of time. We don't prescribe their side of the conversation. We simply wait to hear what they say and then respond to their moves.

Conversations aren't scripts that we read; they're real-life exchanges between two people. The goal is connection, not conversion.

We replace assumptions with truth. When our view of ourselves is based on the opinions of others, we set ourselves up for failure and frustration. Our self-esteem and our identity become the products of how other people see us. That's unhealthy, because we give away the ownership of our emotions as we try to please others.

It's even tougher when we make assumptions about how other people view us. They haven't told us that we're boring or irritating or inferior, but we've decided that they must feel that way. This is often a reflection of how we see ourselves. The downward spiral continues, because we believe our inaccurate assumptions and let them shape our view of ourselves.

Truth is the basis for a healthy self-esteem. Making assumptions about how others view us turns us into people pleasers. Since our opinions of ourselves are based on whether people like us or not, we do everything we can to make them like us. In the process, we give up who we really are.

We replace selfishness with synergy. Synergy is a combination of determination and compassion. Determination means we have the integrity to stand up for our own needs, while compassion means we're committed to addressing the best interests of the other person.

In tough conversations, people with determination alone are committed to getting a satisfying outcome for themselves and don't care whether or not the other person is satisfied. They're not necessarily rigid about their opinions or insisting on being right. But their priority is achieving a solution they can be excited about, not one they have to settle for. This is a selfish perspective and doesn't lead toward resolution of tough conversations.

A person with compassion alone is interested only in making sure the other person is satisfied with the solution. They do what they can to make sure that happens, often at the expense of their own wishes. Such people often give in to the other person so they can avoid conflict. This is a weak perspective and always makes relationships lopsided.

The goal is for both people to be compassionate as well as determined to find a satisfying solution that works well for themselves and the other person. That's a healthy approach because both people are working as a team to achieve a good outcome. That's synergy.

We replace pride with humility. When we believe our perspective is the only accurate one, we can ignore the opinions of others. Such pride can get in the way of effective communication. Humility means we hold our positions loosely while exploring the views of another person.

If we have strong opinions that are different from those of the other person, we can easily focus our energy on the other person instead of on the issue, thinking they're wrong and we're right. Even if we see some validity in their position, we don't want to admit it because it would feel like a sign of weakness. Humility doesn't mean they're right and we're wrong. It means that the relationship is more important than the issue. Pride keeps us from talking honestly because we're unwilling to explore beyond our own opinion. When that happens, connecting stops. Humility is at the base of all effective conversations—especially tough ones.

Prioritizing Relationships

If our identity is based on what others think of us, we don't want anyone to think poorly of us. So we put a lot of energy into making sure everybody likes us. We make choices based on their interests, not our own. That can wear us out.

Technology can make the situation worse, because there are more ways to connect with people than ever before. That means we have a lot more people to stay connected with and impress.

When I signed up for Facebook, I heard from people I hadn't seen for decades. Many were friends from high school or college, and they sent friend requests. I accepted many of the requests because those people had been good friends in the past and I wanted to reconnect. (In reality, I think many people connect just to see what their friends look like after all these years.)

Social media drops many people into our lives. If we're not careful, we can have more people in our lives than we can handle. Since they were friends in the past, we might feel obligated to maintain those friendships at the same level they were before. We're letting them come over to our side of the checkerboard instead of taking ownership of our moves. But we have only a limited bandwidth for relationships. If we try to stay well connected with everyone, we dilute each relationship.

So what should we do? Do we need to ignore those people? No, we need to prioritize them. We need to decide who gets our best attention and who gets less. The closer they are to us, the more attention they deserve. Our spouses and immediate families are the relationships we should be the most committed to, so our connection with them comes first. That's who we spend the most time with, and tough conversations with them matter most. If we spread our emotional energy too thin, we won't have enough energy to maintain our critical relationships. Taking ownership means we make the decisions about who we converse with, and what that communication looks like.

We're the ones who have to decide who else gets our attention and how much (we have to determine the priority and order):

- close friends
- extended family
- work associates
- neighbors
- church and community connections
- customers and clients
- social media contacts
- friends from the past

I found several old high school friends on Facebook who I've reconnected with because they were valuable friends in the past. We stay on each other's radar but don't spend hours on social media with each other. We comment into each other's lives occasionally, which is appropriate.

Others post often and try to rebuild those past relationships and seem hurt that I don't respond in the same way. It's not that those people don't have value; they're just lower on my priority list. I don't want to sacrifice my current relationships for those from the past. I'm responsible for owning my choices, not them.

I used to feel guilty when I didn't stay in touch with people I was so close to in the past. But some people come into our lives for a season, and then we both move on. That's okay. We become new people in new places.

Practical Steps for Taking Ownership

So when it comes to tough conversations, what can we do to stay on our own side of the checkerboard?

- Recognize that when relationships change, our communication patterns need to change as well.
- Accept that we can't change others, but we can influence them.
- Decide not to base our self-worth on the opinions of other people.
- Remember that healthy relationships need healthy people who are independent, not codependent.
- Determine not to be a victim of other people.
- Understand that we're responsible for us. They're responsible for them.

If we take ownership of ourselves, we'll be in the perfect place to have tough conversations when they're needed.

7

Tool #4—Your Personal Fuel Station (Emotions)

> When dealing with people, let us remember we are
> not dealing with creatures of logic. We are dealing
> with creatures of emotion.
>
> Dale Carnegie[1]

If you touch a spark to gasoline, it explodes. Is that good or bad? If it happens inside a piston of your car's engine, it's good. If it happens in your garage, it's bad. Gasoline can be a powerful resource. It allows us to drive across town or fly around the world. We complain about the cost when it goes too high, yet we'll wait in line at the gas pump to fill our tanks. Many world governments are trying to find alternate sources of energy. But until something better comes along, our lives would look a whole lot different if we ran out of gasoline.

At the same time, we know the devastation that can take place if we don't respect its power. We go out of our way to store it properly, dispense it safely, and use it cautiously. Gasoline isn't the problem; it's just a source of energy. The problem comes when it isn't used properly and with control.

Emotions are the same way. We like them when they're good and avoid them when they're bad. In our most important relationships, they can be the source of tremendous joy or unspeakable pain. When things are going well, we love the emotion that makes the connection positive. But when things become tense, we dread the feelings that accompany conflict.

Our spouse is frustrated with something we didn't do; our boss criticizes a report we submitted; a co-worker takes credit for an idea we shared with them; a neighbor gets upset at the leaves in their yard from our tree. Emotion creeps into otherwise stable relationships, and the conversations get tense. We just can't have normal communication when that happens. Tough conversations need a tough strategy.

When those tough times come, the fight-or-flight instinct kicks in. We're uncomfortable. The situation doesn't feel good. We want it to end. So we either fight and use force to get the other person to comply, or we use flight to withdraw from the conflict. Both responses are natural but unhealthy. They both come from seeing emotion as negative, something that needs to be eliminated.

The problem is one of perspective. Emotions aren't good or bad; they're just fuel for our relationships. When controlled and channeled, they provide the passion needed to help relationships grow and mature. When uncontrolled, they can tear relationships apart.

If we try to deny emotions, we eliminate the fuel in our relationships. Without fuel, we get stuck on the side of the road and can't go anywhere. Many couples have had that experience when a spouse becomes emotionally distant. The spouse tries to appear calm and unruffled on the outside, thinking it's a sign of strength and self-control. But the relationship is slowing down because it's running out of fuel. The other spouse says, "I don't care what you feel—just feel *something.*"

The same thing happens when we work for someone who keeps a poker face in conversations. They're unemotional and detached, and it's hard to communicate with them. The emotion is always there, because bosses aren't exempt from emotion. But if we can't tell what they're feeling, we find it tough to have a real conversation. The fuel is gone.

Ignoring emotions doesn't make them go away. Anger doesn't diminish when it's kept inside; it grows like a fungus in a petri dish. The longer it stays buried, the faster and uglier it grows. We think we're being cool, calm, and collected, but we're draining the energy out of our relationships. We've punched a hole in our emotional fuel tank and don't realize that the fuel is leaking out.

The key isn't eliminating or denying our emotions. The key is learning what to do with them.

Does Logic Trump Emotion?

Have you ever tried to use logic when someone was being emotional? How did that go?

When Diane and I were first married, she would come to me, describe a situation that was upsetting her, and tell me the details. Naturally, I assumed she was looking for a solution. Since I was an objective observer, it was easy for me to suggest a course of action to solve the problem. I would try to help by giving advice. From my perspective, the answer was logical. Just do A and B, and you'll end up with C.

That didn't go well. She didn't need advice; she needed me to listen. (We'll devote an entire chapter to listening later.) When I listened to her, my action helped her process her emotion. Once the emotion had been dealt with, she was more than ready to have a conversation about possible solutions.

Using logic when someone is emotional just doesn't work. The problem isn't the logic; it's the timing. Logic becomes valuable after we've processed the emotion. This doesn't apply just to negative emotion. Even strong positive emotion makes us deaf to logic.

When I was in college, I spent several years doing wedding photography. I worked for a popular studio in Phoenix and was partnered with a mentor to learn the ropes. I would shadow the main photographer while he worked a wedding, and he would describe what he was doing and why it was important.

One time he said, "Always watch the bride and groom when they're in the receiving line." (This was in the day when the entire wedding party would line up, and guests would have to shake hands with everyone in the line on their way to congratulating the bride and groom.) "There will often be some little old lady who breaks into the line, goes up to the bride, and starts giving her advice. She'll tell her to watch out for her new husband, because she really doesn't know him yet. She'll warn the bride that after the honeymoon, he'll change—and she needs to be ready for it."

I saw it happen a number of times. Always the bride would be gracious and say, "Oh, thank you so much. I really appreciate the advice." But it was obvious she forgot what was said as soon as the next person in line greeted her. Even if she appreciated the advice, it fell on deaf ears. The bride's emotion was too high to hear logic. It was positive emotion, but it still got in the way.

A Conversation Matrix

Everybody's different. We each have a unique blend of temperament, conversational style, background, and pattern of communicating. When we're having a challenging conversation, we often don't know what style we're dealing with. It feels like we're walking through a zoo when wild animals have escaped. Each one has to be handled differently if we want to survive.

Many books have been written about the different communication styles and temperaments, and they provide valuable information. For our purposes in dealing with tough conversations, we'll broadly combine two types of *people* and two types of *responses*:

1. Are they *extroverts* or *introverts*?
2. Do they tend to operate from *anger* or *fear*?

To learn how to communicate with people, we need to see these four categories in a conversation matrix.

When tough conversations occur and emotions rise, people can feel threatened. Their responses tend to fall into one of two categories: anger or fear.

Anger-based people fight in conflict. Their temperament tends to be more competitive and aggressive, and their natural response is to try to win the argument. They might manipulate the conversation without even realizing it, because their position seems so logical through their eyes. If the other person can't see their logic, they think, "What's wrong with you? It's so obvious!" They gravitate toward anger and forcefulness. Simply stated, they *attack* the problem (and sometimes the person).

Fear-based people use flight in conflict. They tend to turn away from conflict because they're afraid where it might lead.

97

They don't know how to respond in the moment, and they become intimidated. They just want the conflict to be over. If the other person uses logic, it isn't logical to them because they're feeling emotion so strongly about the issue or the encounter. Simply stated, they *avoid* the problem.

The real challenge comes when an anger person is in a tough conversation with a fear person. The anger person is primarily concerned about solving the issue. The fear person is focused on ending the conflict. Both get stuck thinking the other person just doesn't understand their perspective.

Often, the real issue is a difference in temperament. Some people are more extroverted, while others tend to be more introverted. It's not about being shy or outgoing; it's about how we process information.

Extroverts tend to form their thoughts by talking. They're energized by being around other people and need to engage in conversation to determine what they think about something.

Introverts need time to process their thoughts in order to form them. They usually function well in groups but get their energy by spending time alone. They listen to what others say, then need time by themselves to think through the issues before deciding what they think.

Extroverts tend to think faster, while introverts tend to think deeper. Introverts often feel intimidated by extroverts because they don't know how to respond in the moment. They think of the perfect response about ten minutes after the conversation is over. Extroverts often think that since introverts don't answer right away, they don't have a valid position.

Which one is right? Neither one; they're just different. One of the keys to emotional control during tough conversations is to understand the other person's temperament and accept the reality of it. We think, "Why can't they just be like me?" It's because they're not us; they're them.

	Anger	Fear
Extrovert	1 High Energy	2 High Anxiety
Introvert	3 Quiet Resentment	4 Quiet Resignation

Using our conversation matrix, we can discern the unique conversational style and needs of each person we talk to.

Quadrant 1. This person doesn't shy away from tough conversations and often will press for resolution. To an introvert, they might be intimidating. To another extrovert, they might be challenging. We call this the quadrant of high energy because there tends to be passion around any topic.

In high energy conversations, it's important to realize that the thoughts being expressed are probably being shaped in the moment and come out of what the person is feeling. The book of Proverbs says, "A gentle answer turns away wrath" (Prov. 15:1 NASB). To keep a high energy person from monopolizing the direction of the conversation, we need to respond graciously and calmly and not feel rushed to respond. "It's obvious you have strong feelings about this," we might say. "I appreciate you sharing them. I want to think through what you've said, and I'll need a little time to process."

Quadrant 2. This person is quick to share their thoughts and will voice their concerns easily. They're more focused on the problem than the solution and tend to be worried and pessimistic in their communicating. It can be tough to reason with them because of their great concern. We call this the quadrant of high anxiety because emotion often clouds their logic in the moment.

When conversing with a quadrant 2 person, we need to realize their thoughts are still being formed, so we need to avoid assuming that they have a carefully crafted position. If we respond immediately, we may address the wrong issues, because the apparent issues are based on their thoughts at the moment. The more they talk, the more they might clarify or change their position. To engage a high anxiety person, we need to ask them to describe their concerns and listen without countering anything they say. Taking time to understand and explore their concerns tends to lessen the emotions they're feeling, because they have a chance to express them. Once that happens, they'll usually be more open to discussing logic and solutions.

Quadrant 3. People who operate in this quadrant might be hard to read. They have strong emotions but haven't processed their opinions yet. They don't want to express half-baked ideas and sound foolish, so they keep them inside during the tough conversation. They might take a passive-aggressive approach to the issue, pretending that everything is okay. That's why we call this quadrant quiet resentment.

If we can recognize the need for this person to process their thoughts and feelings, we won't push for an immediate response. That type of approach leads to resentment, because they're feeling the pressure to give a quick opinion that's not formed yet. A better response might be, "It seems like you've got some strong feelings about this. I really would like to explore your thoughts and hear your perspective sometime. Would you like to think through them for a couple of days and then get back together?" That's a refreshing option for a quadrant 3 thinker and gives them permission to ponder without dropping into resentment.

Quadrant 4. It might seem like talking to a quadrant 4 person is a conversation with no fuel, because there's not a lot of energy. They haven't formed their opinion because they haven't had time to process, and they tend to focus on everything that could go wrong. It's easy for them to slip into a type of depression and worry. It's also easy for them just to give up to avoid conflict, which is why this is called quiet resignation.

In this quadrant, we need to recognize the reality of what's happening. "I'm guessing there's a lot more to what you're thinking than what I'm hearing, correct?" we could say. "I want to make sure I'm not missing anything important that you're concerned about. Can we talk about this some more in a couple of days?" If we free them up to process without pressure, we make it easier for them to have hope.

Emotion as a Trigger

When relationships get challenging, it's easy to see emotion as the enemy. Anger or fear seems to get in the way of resolving an issue. But emotions shouldn't scare us off, because they're not the problem. Something happened that set off the emotion. We need to figure out what happened and deal with it.

When we see or feel strong emotion, it should become a trigger for us to refocus on the problem that caused it, not a reason to attack the other person. Hurting the other person won't solve the problem, and it postpones finding a solution. If not dealt with, the emotion can fuel a fire that grows out of control and destroys the relationship. If we let emotion get between us, it drives us apart. We need to separate ourselves from the emotion and face it together.

Everybody Feels

Everything we've talked about in this chapter applies to any relationship, whether it's a marriage, a friendship, a family relationship, or a work relationship.

Our relationship with our spouse goes through the same stages as our relationship with our boss, co-worker, extended family member, or neighbor. They all have similar dynamics and go through the same stages. The longer we're in those relationships, the easier it is for emotions to escalate.

But emotion is simply fuel. We're not trying to get rid of the fuel; we're trying to control the burn. If there's no emotion in a relationship, whether positive or negative, the relationship probably isn't worth pursuing.

Practical Steps for Channeling Emotions

Emotions are vital for healthy communication. It's easier to channel strong emotion than to run a relationship with the tank on empty. How can we take control of the emotional energy when conversations get tough? We need to focus on these steps:

- *Don't ignore or cover emotions.* We need to talk about them with the other person and bring them out in the open.
- *Recognize that emotions aren't good or bad; they just are.*
- *Realize that emotionless conversation is just chatting.* Rich emotions are the fuel for rich connections, especially when conversations get tough.
- *Become a student of each person we encounter.* We need to learn their temperament and conversational style, then craft our approach to meet their needs.
- *Celebrate differences.* We should strive for synergy, not sameness.

8

Tool #5—Crock-Pot Relationships (Time)

Come on, inner peace—I don't have all day. . . .

Anonymous

Before television came into our lives, we knew that relationships took time to build and problems took time to solve. There were no shortcuts; we had to talk to each other and work through real issues over time. When a quarrel happened in a family, there were strong emotions and tough conversations. But this was expected. We also understood that healing took time.

But television changed our perspective. Here's what we learned in those early days of television:

- Every relationship has drama.
- That drama can be solved in sixty minutes (minus commercials) and results in a happy ending.

About that same time, we discovered instant oatmeal, instant rice, instant pudding, and instant coffee. Microwaves came along some time later, which we could buy on instant credit. It was an age of convenience. As long as we were willing to pay for it, anything we wanted could happen quickly in this modern society.

As a result, we have become impatient. Now we use our phones to find just about any information we need. When a website takes a second or two to load, we switch to another site. Add the fact that we have more to do than ever before in history, and we have a recipe for disaster. We're overworked, overstimulated, and overwhelmed. We have a ton of stuff that "needs" to get done, so we utilize our time management skills and best technology to work at top speed.

In most areas of life, that might help us become more effective—but not in relationships. There's no such thing as an instant deep relationship. Relationships happen in the Crock-Pot, not the microwave.

What Time Management Hurts the Most

I've been teaching productivity seminars—time management—for the past twenty-five years. That's over three thousand classes. Here's what I've learned:

- We all have twenty-four hours a day, and that's it.
- We can't manage time. We can only manage the choices we make during the passage of time.
- Most time-management courses focus on getting everything done and doing it right.
- It's better to focus on getting the right things done.

Over the years, I've watched people get excited about time management. They learn new tools and techniques for accomplishing tasks and getting more things checked off their to-do lists. Time management actually works; their piles get smaller, and their desks get cleaner.

It feels good to get more done. We feel more productive, which makes us feel more valuable, which makes us feel better about ourselves. That can be addictive. When we see these techniques working, we think, "If I just work a little harder at them, I can become even more productive." These thoughts begin to filter into other areas of our lives. We develop a mindset of productivity and look for ways to do everything faster and more efficiently. We sleep less and work more.

While we're increasing our productivity, there's a downside to being efficient. In fact, in one area of life, productivity and efficiency can be counterproductive: our communication.

The more efficient we try to be with our important relationships and the more we try to rush through tough issues, the more our relationships suffer and the longer resolution takes. That can be frustrating, because it feels like the other person isn't cooperating. After all, everything else in life works well by doing it quicker. Why not our conversations?

The thing that makes conversations effective is the opposite of efficiency. Relationships don't grow when we have quick, planned conversations. Real conversations happen spontaneously on the porch or in the break room, in quiet times, when we're slogging through life together. Effectiveness means simply being present in another person's life. Caring is demonstrated through the calendar, not the clock. We can't rush relationships. And we especially can't rush tough conversations.

My wife and I just spent the better part of five days with our three grandchildren while their parents took a trip. Normally, we get to see the kids every couple of weeks for a few hours. But this time, they woke up in our house and went to sleep at our house. They were with us 24/7.

In that time, I learned something. When we're with them for a few hours, we're catching up with them—hearing about school and their friends, seeing the pictures they've drawn, and playing together. We love those times; it's a chance to touch base again.

When they were with us all the time, we got to hear their hearts. We didn't have planned conversations in which we asked preplanned questions. We were just being together in the same space for an uninterrupted time.

It's valuable to ask our kids, spouses, friends, and other people who are important to us what they're thinking. We learn a lot that way. But it's also important to spend longer, relaxed time with those important people when we don't have a formal agenda. When we're unhurried, conversational nuggets of gold can be found.

A Recipe for Relationships

It's tough to have uninterrupted, quality time with people when the demands of life suck us dry. Work requires long hours, houses need maintenance, and obligations keep us in constant motion. It's like trying to relax during a hurricane. If we want to build connections, we have to discern which things add value and which things are simply distractions.

Goethe said, "Things which matter most must never be at the mercy of things which matter least."[1] I love that. This quotation needs to be on our walls, our screen savers, and our dashboards. I think it would make a seriously good tattoo. It doesn't provide an easy answer, but it reminds us of the need to make good choices, avoiding the distractions that rob our relationships.

Time management tries to fill every moment with productivity. That means we get more done, which sounds like a good thing. But if we fill every available moment trying to get another check mark on our to-do lists, we give away those moments when we can simply be available to the people who matter most to us. Without those moments, we will have a hard time hearing their hearts. Life doesn't happen on schedule. If we keep our schedules too rigid, we lose our margin. We don't have room for human moments.

Someone said, "When you die, there will still be things on your to-do list that you didn't get done. So make sure you do the important things." Those important things make up the recipe for healthy relationships and healthy conversations, and there are three of them.

The First Ingredient: Time

Most people realize that the most secure way to build wealth is to invest early, making small deposits consistently for a long time. Once we develop that habit, the return on our investment grows exponentially over time.

But we can be tempted to take shortcuts. An opportunity to make a quick fortune captures our attention, and it pulls our focus away from the steady commitment we've made. It feels like a sure thing, and nothing can go wrong. It's a no-brainer.

That's the problem: we stop using our brain. Our emotions take over, and we go for the quick reward. Sometimes things work out, but usually we take a detour from the path toward real wealth. Impatience short-circuits our progress, and we lose momentum.

It's tempting to go for quick fixes in tough conversations as well:

- We make promises to our boss that we know aren't realistic, but we want him to feel good about us in the moment.

- We use flattery with a friend to get her to think well of us, when we know it's a toxic relationship.

- We force ourselves to make a phone call to someone to keep them from getting upset rather than as an expression of true friendship.

- We feel obligated to spend time with our spouse or family member to pretend that the relationship is healthy. We don't want to, and we're relieved when the time is over.

Quick fixes are like putting a bandage on a broken arm. There's no superglue for broken relationships. Building, healing, and maintaining relationships comes from unhurried, genuine conversations.

The Second Ingredient: Intention

There's no substitute for time in any relationship. But just spending time isn't enough. I spend hours next to people on airplanes, but there's no relationship. We also need to be intentional with the other person, truly focused on their uniqueness and their needs.

I can spend hours with you, but our relationship won't grow if I spend the entire time talking about myself. The only way we'll build a real connection is if I genuinely want to know you on the inside. I want to look through your eyes and see what you see. I can't pretend to be interested; it has to be genuine. I have to be intentional.

People think that social media is the perfect way to stay in touch with many friends. There's some truth to that, because it does keep us on each other's radar. But it also has its limitations. With social media, I can send notes to ten people in one hour. I feel productive, like I've made wise use of my time. But social media also has the feel of a checklist, where I'm trying to see how many people I can touch base with as quickly as possible.

If I spend that same hour with one person at a coffee shop, I won't get as many check marks. I won't feel as efficient. But I will have the opportunity to intentionally connect with someone at a deeper level, and the communication will move forward.

There's a definite place for social media, but it's not for making deep connections with people and growing relationships. It's for keeping track of others in a casual way, much like we read the newspaper to get an overview of what's happening in the world. The return on our investment of time is minimal. Quick conversations are like putting coins in a vending machine. Once we turn the dial, the coins are gone forever (and the gumball lasts only a few minutes).

Intentional time spent face-to-face is like investing in a high-quality financial portfolio. Those small deposits made consistently over time can produce a huge dividend for the future. We build trust and understanding between ourselves and others, and commitment grows. The return on our investment can grow exponentially, providing a solid connection for the future.

The Third Ingredient: Patience

During my college years, I stood in the Sistine Chapel while on a trip to Italy. I remember being amazed at the intensity of the ceiling, awestruck by the realism of the frescoes and the detail. It's always humbling to stand in the presence of a masterpiece.

I was even more fascinated with the details of Michelangelo's four-year effort to produce the work of art. Normally, we think of an artist being inspired, almost in a spiritual trance as they transfer that creativity to their canvas. Creating a piece of art doesn't sound like work; it sounds like soul expression.

Michelangelo didn't see it that way. He saw himself as a sculptor, not a painter. He was working on marble sculptures for the pope's tomb when the pope commissioned him to do the painting. He was reluctant but felt he had no choice. So he began the work.

He erected a wooden scaffold at one end of the chapel, attaching timbers to holes near the windows instead of building from the ground up. Most people think of him lying on his back the entire time, which would make sense. But he actually stood on the scaffolding, craning his neck back to work overhead. (Our image of him lying down came from Charlton Heston in the movie *The Agony and the Ecstasy* years ago.)

His technique involved applying wet plaster in small sections, then coloring those sections as they dried. It didn't go well at first, because the dampness in the plaster produced mold in the earlier sections. Michelangelo had to scrape it off and start over. When inspiration was lacking, he made up for it with patience.

Michelangelo wanted to stop repeatedly. He even wrote a poem about his misery during the process, describing the pain his body was in and how he wasn't a true painter. For four years, he did the hard work to produce a masterpiece. In contrast, near the end, he painted the figure of God in the act of creation in a single day.[2]

Centuries later, millions of people file through the Vatican to experience the majesty of Michelangelo's work. If he had used a color-by-number template or whipped the ceiling out in a week, no one would notice. But he exercised patience to fight through the tough times, and the results are legendary. Originals require time and patience to produce but have great value. Copies can be mass-produced quickly and casually, and can be bought for pennies at garage sales.

Relationships that have the greatest value can't be rushed. People have done the hard work to make them happen. When patience runs out in relationships, people run out of quality relationships. Valuable relationships are built on patience and the commitment to keep working on them when things get tough.

When our kids were infants, we spent a lot of time changing their diapers. We're talking cloth diapers, not disposables. So that meant swishing those messy diapers in the toilet, putting them in a hamper filled with bleach water, and laundering the entire mess on a regular basis.

Years later, in a moment of boredom, I tried to estimate how many times we had changed diapers over those years. I don't remember the exact number, but it was over ten thousand times for two kids.

That took patience—and commitment. There were times when we would get them all cleaned up, change their diaper, and they would immediately soil it again. It was like the clean diaper was a trigger that would set their little systems in motion. It was frustrating, and tried our patience. We longed for the day when they could take care of business on their own, but we knew it would simply take time.

It's natural to have patience with babies, because we know they won't become mature overnight. But with adults, we get impatient when they don't respond in mature ways immediately. We forget that we're all in process.

Time, intention, and patience are the ingredients for solid relationships that can weather the storms that inevitably come. Tough conversations are just that: tough. Hanging in there during those tough times is how valuable relationships become priceless.

Making Good Choices

Someone said that good habits are hard to form but easy to break. Bad habits are easy to form but hard to break.

It's human nature to take the path of least resistance. When faced with two choices, we gravitate toward the easy instead of the hard. If I'm offered a plate of celery or a plate of warm cookies, I'll take the cookies every time (unless you're watching). Someone might say, "Just make the best choice. No one's forcing you to eat the cookies. Just eat the celery." But there's more going on. Celery doesn't stir up cravings inside of me. Warm cookies smell better than cold celery.

Examples like that break down, because they assume we have only two choices. In real life, we can be creative in the moment. Resisting the cookies might still be a tough choice, but it will be a lot easier if I replace the celery with one of my favorite foods that's actually healthy.

We have an easier time resisting if we've developed healthy habits ahead of time. Individual choices in the moment always involve willpower. Better choices are part of a pattern that has developed over time.

When our most valuable relationships go through challenging times, we have the tendency to pull away. Facing tough conversations feels like facing that plate of celery; we'll take the easy way out of a tough conversation by withdrawing, accusing, or verbally attacking the other person.

The only way we'll be able to make healthy choices in conversation is if we understand the value of the relationship. Making little deposits in that relationship over time adds up to a large return on our investment. Over time, there's a good chance those deposits can influence someone's behavior.

There's No Instant Maturity

Every relationship will have its rough spots where conversations become uncomfortable and challenging. Tough times are normal, no matter how healthy a relationship is. Trying to use quick fixes during those times is unproductive, because doing so sabotages the long-term growth.

There have been times when I've thought, "I wish I could live my life over again, knowing what I know now. I would have done things differently."

I can't go there. Back then, I simply didn't have the knowledge I have now. It took years of living to get that knowledge. It took time, and I had to get where I am one day at a time.

There are no shortcuts to maturity. There are no shortcuts to healthy relationships. Maturity takes time. Once we accept that reality, we're free to experience our relationships in the present. Instead of wishing the other person would change now, we make our investments in the moment. Over time, we'll see the payoff. But the biggest payoff always comes in the future, not the present.

When tough conversations happen, we'd love to handle them perfectly. It's not going to happen. We need to use the tools we have in the moment instead of wishing for tools that will come as we grow. When that happens, we can be honest in the moment instead of dreaming about the future.

Growth takes time. It's worth pursuing because of what maturity brings to our relationships and our conversations. But that growth doesn't happen overnight. It happens as we make small, consistent investments in our relationships.

Starting now.

Practical Steps for Using Time Wisely

Since we can't make more time, we have to make wise choices about the time we have. Here are some reminders:

- We can't rush relationships—or the tough conversations that go along with them.

- It's easy to get distracted from the things that matter most.
- When a conversation gets challenging, we need to spend quality time with each other instead of efficiently texting our thoughts.
- Small emotional deposits over time result in huge emotional reserves.

9

Tool #6—The Value of Everybody (Respect)

> Respect old people. They graduated high school
> without Google or Wikipedia.
>
> Anonymous

Last year, your daughter's elementary school teacher was awesome, and your daughter was motivated to learn. This year, you wonder how this teacher got her credentials, and your daughter is bored and falling behind. You've tried to reason with the teacher, but she just doesn't seem to hear you. You're upset, but you're also stuck. You can't change teachers. What should you do? You know there's a tough conversation coming—with her? With the principal? With your daughter?

How can we respect someone who doesn't deserve it?

That's a tough question but an important one. Respect is the lubricant of any relationship. When it's present, everything else runs smoother. When it's absent, everything else is rougher. Respect isn't just for what someone does; it's about who they are. When someone has high character and donates a million dollars to an orphanage, we respect them. But if a person of low character does the same thing, we're happy for the orphanage—but we don't respect the person.

So what is respect? How do we get it, and how do we keep it? And how do we develop respect for others, especially in the midst of tough conversations?

The Case for Respect

I once heard someone describe respect as "showing appreciation for the worth of someone." That's an interesting perspective, because it focuses on the innate value of others, not their performance. It says, "You have value simply because you're you." So if you perform well, you have value. If you mess up, you have value. You have innate value simply because you exist on the planet.

I'm always amazed at how much disrespect people can have for others because of their beliefs, even if they don't know the person. When someone disagrees with them, they can almost develop a hatred for that person.

Yesterday, I drove by our local post office. On the street corner, a tall woman stood near a small table surrounded by handmade signs and pictures of the president of the United States. She had drawn a small moustache on him to identify him with Adolf Hitler and written slogans that expressed her anger at what she perceived he was doing to our country. Apparently, her anger had been building up to the point that she simply had to take it public. I wondered how someone could develop such hatred for someone she had probably never met.

I didn't stop to talk with her, primarily because I wasn't interested in a lengthy discussion about politics. Her signs were filled with venom. She was obviously on a mission to convince everyone she could how evil the president was and to turn people against him. In those kinds of situations, arguing is pointless.

On a lesser scale, we see the same thing in sporting events. People begin to heckle the opposing fans. Add a few drinks, and they become vicious. They don't know the other fans, but they have developed anger toward them because they're cheering for the opponent. How can people feel this way toward others when they don't even know them? They dehumanize them. They don't see them as real people; they simply see them as the enemy.

We might experience the same thing when we're driving. Someone cuts us off or makes a crazy lane change without signaling, and we form an opinion of their character. Since we don't know who they are, we usually see them as a combination of all the worst people we know.

But what about someone we know, like a spouse, family member, or boss? It's much harder to disrespect someone we're close to. We have to separate ourselves emotionally from them in order to treat them with contempt. In a sense, we dehumanize them. We can justify our anger if the other person has no value in our eyes.

Hug a Server Today

I spend a lot of time in hotel meeting rooms. As I'm getting ready for a session, service personnel are setting up tables and equipment, arranging food, and tidying up the room. During breaks, they swoop in and clear dirty dishes, remove trash from tables, and reset the room for the next segment. They work quietly but proficiently. Their job is to make the experience as positive as possible for participants so nothing gets in the way of the focus of the day.

Those people are invisible. At the end of the day, I could ask anyone in my seminar to describe one of these workers, and I probably wouldn't find anyone who could do it. They'll go home and talk about all the interesting people they met. But they can't remember even seeing one of the serving staff, much less interacting with them.

That's unfortunate, because they miss some great opportunities. These servers are generally proud of the work they do, and they want to make a good experience for everyone. They're not looking to be in the limelight; they're content to be in the shadows, working with excellence. I've heard some fascinating stories when I've taken the time to interact with them.

The same thing is true in a restaurant. Overlooking the servers might not be as obvious, because they're paid to interact with customers. Some customers see them as real people and interact with them as such. Others see them as hired servants, paid to wait on them and do what they ask. If there's a problem with the service, they berate the server and write a scathing review on social media review sites.

How can they treat servers with such disrespect? By dehumanizing them—seeing them as invisible instead of as real people.

We don't respect things; we respect people. When we stop respecting people, we turn them into things.

Respect is one of the foundations of effective relationships and strong communication—and it's essential for handling tough conversations. Respect challenges us in at least two ways:

1. learning to respect ourselves
2. developing respect for others

Learning to Respect Ourselves

We have a tendency to base our self-worth on the opinions of other people. If they like us, we feel good about ourselves. If they don't like us, we doubt ourselves. When we do that, we give away the ownership of our lives to other people. We're dependent on them for our value. We become like a boat with no engine, drifting wherever the current takes us.

Answer these questions to see if you've given that control away to others:

- Do you find it difficult to say no to people's requests, even if you know those requests aren't in your best interest?
- Do you often feel like others take advantage of you?
- Do people seem to overlook the positive things you do for them, taking you for granted?
- Do you always get the work assignments nobody else wants to do?
- Do you keep your opinions to yourself when you disagree with someone in order to avoid conflict?
- Do you take care of others more than you take care of yourself?
- Do you go along with others when you don't feel like it because you don't want them to think badly of you?

If you answered yes to most of these questions, it's probably time to take back the control of your life.

Respecting ourselves means we set healthy boundaries. We don't automatically comply with the wishes of other people; we choose what we do instead of letting others decide. We stand up for what we believe. We learn how to say no.

We need to pay attention to what we say to ourselves about ourselves. When we catch negative self-talk happening, we need to corral those thoughts and ask ourselves if they're accurate. If they're not, we need to let them go and replace them with truth.

Developing Respect for Others

When conversations get tough, we often respond by digging in our heels and fighting for our position, hoping to convince the other person they're wrong. These kinds of conversations tend to escalate, because we're focused on ourselves and what we want. Respect for each other goes out the window, because we each think the other person is the problem.

If we can learn to maintain respect for the other person in the midst of conflict, we have an opportunity for realistic, healthy dialogue. That's hard when we're upset. Respect is a choice we can make, even in the middle of strong emotion.

How can we choose respect? We begin by making sure we don't dehumanize the other person. We see them as they really are, a flawed individual who makes good choices and bad choices. In other words, they're just like us.

The more important the relationship is, the more important it is to keep respect in our conversations. For the purpose of the tough conversation, we're both on the same team trying to reach a common goal. Respect allows us to attack the problem instead of each other.

When Respect Is Nonexistent

This book is about tough conversations. We're talking about relationships that are important to us, where it's worth the effort and the risk to communicate effectively.

Sometimes the relationship has become toxic. Respect is nonexistent, and people in toxic relationships see each other as less than human—which allows them to become vicious with each other.

Communication problems at this level are beyond the scope of this book because there are deeper issues. Solving them is not a matter of learning better conversational skills; there is a relational issue. In those situations, we need professional help. We are often reluctant to see a therapist or counselor, feeling that it means we've failed. Our pride makes us want to be able to fix everything ourselves.

When things need fixing around our house, my wife and I usually do the work ourselves. Sometimes we know what we're doing. Other times we're in over our heads, so we go to our local home repair store and ask for advice.

When something goes wrong that involves the electrical system, I call a professional. I know it's dangerous to do the work myself. Asking for help doesn't make me feel like a failure. I'm more concerned with staying alive.

I wouldn't attempt to do my own brain surgery to save money. I'd want to have the best brain surgeon in the business. That doesn't mean I'm weak; it means the problem is bigger than my skills. When a relationship has become toxic, a gifted counselor, psychologist, or therapist can move us toward healing in ways we can't accomplish on our own.

The bottom line is that respect is crucial in any relationship that's important to us. Without it, the relationship crumbles over time. When it's present, it provides a foundation to build on. It helps us work as a team to attack the issue rather than attacking each other. Respect reminds us of what's really most important: the relationship.

Practical Steps for Maintaining Respect

How do we show respect for a person when we're upset with them?

- We fight with fairness and accuracy (no exaggerations).
- We don't belittle them.

- We listen.
- We don't use absolutes ("You *never* . . . You *always* . . .").
- We don't attack their character.
- We tell the truth.
- We don't interrupt.
- We work hard to understand their perspective, even if we don't agree with it.
- We're patient instead of forcing a quick solution.
- We don't talk negatively about them behind their back.
- We control our emotions rather than letting our emotions control us.
- We don't get defensive. That ends effective dialogue.

Skills for Healthy Conversations

Several years ago, I came across an announcement for an "Ultimate Workshop" sweepstakes. If I submitted my name and was chosen, I would win a collection of tools that would make any craftsman salivate. The collection included every tool I could ever wish for—power tools, hand tools, auto tools, and the cabinets to hold them all. There were hundreds of tools included in the grand prize.

"If I had all those tools," I thought, "I could build anything. I would be a master craftsman."

The problem is that having the "ultimate workshop" or the "ultimate kitchen" or the "ultimate gym" isn't enough. The tools won't do anything by themselves; they have to be put to use by someone who knows what they're doing. It doesn't matter how good my tools are if I have no woodworking skills. A dream kitchen is useless if I don't know anything about cooking. I can get hurt with exercise equipment if I don't know how to work out.

Half of any project is having the right tools. The other half is knowing what to do with them.

In previous chapters, we've picked up the tools for healthy conversations. Now we need to learn how to use them. In this section, we'll explore six skills that utilize the tools in our toolbox:

1. make it safe
2. eliminate intimidation
3. practice power listening
4. encourage honest feedback
5. start with kindness
6. know your purpose

These aren't the only skills, but they're foundational. If we practice them regularly, we'll have the potential for relationships in which effective communication thrives.

Keep your toolbox handy, and let's explore these critical skills for using our tools effectively.

10

Skill #1—Make It Safe

Fear is an emotion people like to feel when they know they're safe.

Alfred Hitchcock[1]

Recently, I spent a couple of days training at a company in West Chester, Ohio. During the night, a major thunderstorm hit. The lightning never stopped, and the thunder rattled the walls of the hotel. I love these types of storms and hadn't experienced one like that since I lived in Phoenix.

The next morning, the storm was quite a topic of discussion among the class participants. One woman told me it was the craziest storm she had seen in the past twenty years. Other people remarked how they thought it might have been a tornado in the making and how they had tried to decide if they should go to the basement and take cover.

Someone said, "You live in Southern California, right? So that must have been pretty scary for you." Before I could respond, another person said, "But you have earthquakes. These storms must be nothing compared to an earthquake. How can you stand to live there?"

I replied, "Actually, I'd rather have an earthquake than a tornado or hurricane. With a tornado, you have anticipation. You worry about how close it will get and how bad it will be. With an earthquake, you don't know when it's coming. When it hits, it takes a couple of seconds to realize what's happening. By the time you figure it out, it's usually over. If you're still alive, you're good to go."

Alfred Hitchcock, the film director called "the master of suspense," said, "Suspense and terror cannot coexist."[2] Suspense builds slowly, whereas terror is immediate and unexpected. In his movies, he would build scenes in which viewers sensed something bad was coming, so when it finally happened, it was expected. That's suspense.

Terror, on the other hand, happens when something jumps out of the shadows with no warning and takes our breath away. There's no suspense, just shock. If Hitchcock's audience felt suspense, the element of surprise was gone—so there was no terror.

Hurricanes are suspense. Earthquakes are terror.

Hitchcock capitalized on people's fear. He wrote, "Millions of people every day spend huge sums of money and go to great hardship merely to *enjoy* fear. . . . The boy who walks a tightrope or tiptoes along the top of a picket fence is looking for fear, as are the auto racer, the mountain climber, and the big-game hunter."[3]

Relationship Suspense versus Relationship Terror

Fear isn't found only in Hollywood. Fear impacts everyday relationships as well. When we know our boss believes in us, we can handle the tough conversations when they come. When we fear our job is in jeopardy or that our boss doesn't support us, we lack confidence when conflicts arise.

Every relationship experiences moments of "terror." Unexpected events happen—job losses, family crises, illnesses, accidents, financial issues—and they threaten to destroy our equilibrium. They test the relationship to the limit, showing what that relationship is really made of. These events don't discriminate; they appear in the healthiest and the unhealthiest relationships.

Some relationships are characterized by "suspense." Communication is strained, and both people feel like they're walking on eggshells. They're afraid to bring up tough issues because they're afraid the other person might explode, withdraw, get defensive, or leave. The relationship isn't safe. There's no confidence in the long-term commitment to the relationship.

Other relationships are considered "safe." These people have healthy ways of communicating and are convinced that the other person has their best interests in mind. They don't like tough conversations but are willing to have them when necessary. There's confidence in the commitment each person has to the relationship and to each other, which provides a foundation for deep, honest interaction.

When terror events hit a suspense relationship, they tend to drive a wedge between two people. They don't have the commitment to each other to face the event together, so they each take their best shot at it alone. That drives them apart, because they let the event get between them and push them away from each other. Effective communication disappears.

When terror events hit a safe relationship, they tend to draw two people closer together. They have the commitment to work on the issue as a team. They put the issue outside of them so it pushes them together rather than driving them apart.

How We Determine Safety

We all formed our perspective about safety when we were young. We didn't get to pick our parents, our socioeconomic level, or our location. We didn't have any choice about what kind of discipline we received, whether we were nurtured or not, and what tools we were given for negotiating life. We inherited our environment and the people who came with it.

In that dependent state, we were at the mercy of other people. If we sensed that those people were trustworthy, we formed an impression that the world was a safe place. If we got mixed messages from those people, we sensed that the world was a place for suspicion.

Those impressions provided our earliest tools for handling life—tools we will use the rest of our lives. Those impressions also established our default setting for how we view other people. If we sensed in those early days that people were trustworthy, our default setting as adults will probably be one of trust (until the other person proves otherwise). If we grew up thinking that people were not trustworthy, we will probably view most people we meet with suspicion rather than trust. Whatever tools we acquired are the tools we learned to use. That's why so many people say, "I can't change; that's just the way I am."

But people *can* change. It might not be easy, but it's possible. No matter how we've viewed people in the past, we can choose to see them differently. We start by recognizing what our default setting is from the past, then deciding how to respond differently.

The default setting will always be there, but we can learn to work around it. A computer has a motherboard that runs the operating system for that machine, but the computer can also use software. In the same way, we'll always have the same basic hardware, but we can run different software to make us respond in new ways.

This is an important issue to consider, because every person has a basic need for safety. When it's present in a relationship, everything else is possible. When it's missing, everything else is challenging. Safety provides the foundation that makes a relationship work.

My friend Jim is a structural engineer. When a city decides to build a skyscraper, they hire Jim to do all the work that takes place underground. He makes sure the foundation is absolutely solid, taking into consideration all the characteristics of the earth in which they build. He's the ultimate professional, and contractors trust him. They know that if Jim is responsible for the foundation, they can build fifty or sixty stories without worrying about what will happen. Once the building is finished, no one ever sees his work or even thinks about it. But the solid foundation makes everything possible that happens above the ground.

When we're not sure if our relationship is safe and secure, our conversations become a lot more challenging. When that foundation is solid, we can connect without concern.

How We Grow Safety

I was talking to a utility meter reader a few years ago about dogs. He has spent years entering people's yards and had a list of notes about animals at every house he visits—what kind, whether they are locked up, and if there are any issues related to the dog. He also carries a stick with a rubber ball at the end and has been trained in how to use it to distract a dog if it becomes vicious.

I said, "Have you ever been bitten?"

He said, "Yeah, a few times. But every time it was a little dog. And a few times, it happened right after the homeowner said, 'He's harmless. He doesn't bite.' Then it would clamp onto my leg."

He said that because of his training he isn't afraid of dogs, but he always approaches them cautiously. He assumes each one will bite. After he has a number of encounters with the same dog, he learns if he can trust it or not. He starts with a lens of "vicious" until the dog proves otherwise—at which time he changes his lens to "safe."

In every new relationship, we decide if it's safe or not. Once we decide, that becomes the lens through which we see the relationship. From that point on, we assume the lens is accurate.

If we decide a person is trustworthy, we give them the benefit of the doubt when they mess up. We believe it was a mistake or a poor choice made by a good person. "They didn't mean to do that," we say to ourselves. It's only when they start messing up consistently that we question our lens.

If we decide a person is not trustworthy, we're suspicious of anything they do or say. We question their motives. "They're just trying to make me think they've changed. But it won't work." We'll risk trusting them only after we see consistency in their actions.

To make relationships more complicated, it takes only one major action to break trust with someone, but it takes multiple actions to gain trust again. It's not enough to say, "I'm sorry" when we mess up, though that's the obvious first step. We have to build trust back, and that happens over time through repeated positive actions.

If we want to build safety into a relationship, we need to be intentional about doing the positive things that demonstrate commitment and consistency. The other person has to see that we're serious about making the relationship a priority.

How to Make People Feel Safe

The problem with earthquakes is that we've learned to count on the ground not moving. When it moves, it messes with our security. When the thing we've come to trust gives way, it's unsettling. We don't feel safe.

What does "safe" look like in a relationship? A relationship is safe when people have their needs met by the other person.

We all want to be loved, affirmed, valued, and secure. Even when those needs aren't met, they're still there. If other people don't value us, we find other ways to get their attention.

When I was in high school, I went through the insecurity that many kids go through when they're trying to find their way into adulthood. I wanted people to like me, but I didn't value myself. So I tried to do things to make people like me. I started working at jobs that nobody else did so people would look up to me. I worked in a morgue at a county hospital, sold musical instruments, did offset printing, became a radio announcer, and did wedding photography. People were impressed, but it didn't make me feel better. I got a lot of attention for those things, but I felt like people were only impressed with my actions, not with me.

Here's the problem: If everybody is trying to get their needs met, we're all in a taking mode. We want other people to meet those needs for us. But if everybody is taking and nobody is giving, the entire process spirals downward.

Learning to focus on the needs of others doesn't mean we give up our own needs and become a doormat. It simply means we're intentional about making others feel valued. If we do that, we're helping them find safety at the most basic level. When that need is met, they are free to begin doing the same in return. The result? A foundation is formed for handling tough conversations.

That doesn't mean we manipulate others so they'll meet our needs. We have to have a genuine desire to help someone because we care about them. We can't guarantee how they'll respond, but it puts us in a different mind-set that focuses on giving instead of taking.

What can we do to make others feel safe?

We Draw Them Out

Safety grows when the other person feels that we're genuine in our concern and care for them. One of the best ways to do that is through intentional listening (something we'll cover in an upcoming chapter).

Most people listen to others casually, using their words as a springboard for the next thing they want to say. But the best listeners don't move on to other topics quickly; they explore what the other person has said.

During a conversation, the other person says, "They never listen to me at work. I feel like I'm invisible." A typical response might be, "Yeah, that's happened to me before. I remember one time when . . ." When that happens, we're not listening anymore; we're telling stories about ourselves.

A better response is to stop and draw them out: "When you say you feel invisible, what does that look like? What have people said or done that makes you feel that way?" This level of attention lets the other person know we care enough to explore. We value them and want to look through their eyes to see what they see. We're not trying to fix the situation; we're just coming alongside them in their journey.

We Control Our Responses

When we explode at people or get defensive during tough conversations, the relationship feels unsafe. The emotion isn't the problem, because it's real. The problem is how we express the emotion. Verbally attacking another person makes them feel threatened, not safe. They feel like we're critiquing them instead of the issue.

We can express emotion, but we need to do so with honesty and control. Instead of saying, "You're so stupid. How could you do such a thing?" we might say, "I feel really angry and hurt when you do that. I feel like it's hard to trust you." Uncontrolled emotion during conflict is like pouring gasoline on a fire. It only escalates the conflict. The conflict is the problem, but we make it worse by our approach.

If a spouse or boss is exploding or venting, they stop effective conversation. It's tempting to try to address their style during the confrontation, but that's using logic when someone is emotional. We might have that conversation, but it needs to happen later when everyone is relaxed—not during the emotion of the battle. That's when we could say, "Can we talk about what happened the other day? I really want to make sure we can be honest with each other about tough issues. But I think there's something that might be getting in the way. Can we explore it?" Then we can discuss perspectives rather than getting defensive and attacking each other.

We Clarify Expectations

Your boss says, "I need you to set up a meeting for me with Phil at noon tomorrow." So you call Phil and arrange for him to meet in your boss's office at noon.

When your boss finds out, he says, "I wanted a lunch meeting, not a meeting in my office. It's at noon; that's lunchtime. You'd think that would be obvious."

Did you do what your boss asked? Yes. Was your boss happy? No.

Sure, the boss should have been more clear. But he wasn't, and you did exactly what was asked. The misunderstanding came because the expectations were unclear.

It's easy to assume the boss was at fault and should have been clearer. But we can't control what the boss does. Instead, we need to take the initiative when the assignment is given to clarify those expectations. "Okay, I'll set up a noon meeting. Where would you like to meet? How long is the meeting for? Does he need to do anything to prepare for the meeting?"

It would be nice if everyone was always clear in describing their expectations. But in any relationship, we can only control what we do. If we take the time up front to do the clarification ourselves, we'll save ourselves a lot of potential grief in the future.

We Accept Their Faults

Nobody's perfect, including us. It's easy to be irritated when people do things differently than we would do them, especially when we "know" we're right. But people find safety in a relationship when they know their actions are separated from their value as a person. If they know we accept them for who they are even when they mess up, they feel the safety they need to make the relationship work.

Your husband surprises you by planning dinner. He's not the greatest cook, but he finds a killer recipe to try. The results are . . . well, less than stellar. What do you say?

If you both know the dinner didn't turn out well, admit it. But do it in a way that's honest about both the food and your spouse. "You have no idea how much it means to me that you went to the effort to plan this all out. I know you're not happy with the way it turned out. But it's not about the food. It's about spending time with you. Thanks."

Faults can't be overlooked because they're real and obvious. But they don't define the other person. Relationships are built on honesty between two imperfect people. When we try to make the other person perfect or force them to fit into our image of what they should be like, we sabotage the growth of the relationship.

We Build Boundaries in Our Relationships

As Robert Frost wrote, "Good fences make good neighbors." We might trust the person living next to us, so we don't put up a fence. But when their crabgrass starts to sneak over onto our side of the lawn, we end up dealing with emotional issues. A fence isn't a sign of mistrust; it's a tool for keeping relationships healthy.

When we have a relationship with someone we care about, we protect the relationship from outside forces that might drive us apart. We keep each other's secrets. We don't discuss sensitive issues in public. We don't talk to others to build support when we're irritated with the other person. We talk to them, not others.

When to Fasten Our Seat Belts

When a plane encounters turbulence, the pilot tells the passengers to put on their seat belts. I've noticed that few people actually do it. After all, it's just a little bumpy, not roller-coaster wild.

But as soon as the plane takes a nosedive, the first thing people do is fasten their seat belts. The instructions from the pilot weren't enough, because the problem didn't seem that severe. But when people feel like they're in danger, they start taking precautions.

The longer any relationship continues, the more turbulence the people involved will encounter. There will be major bumps along the way. It's just part of the relationship growing. When those bumps happen, we start looking for solutions. We want to fix the issues, but they've become bigger than we can handle.

The time to put on the seat belt is at the beginning of the flight, not when the turbulence hits. It provides a sense of safety that comes from being prepared.

When people feel safe in a relationship, they have the foundation for handling the turbulence. Safety provides an environment in which long-term growth and maturity can occur. It prepares people for the storm.

Want to feel safe? Now is the time to fasten our seat belts.

Tips for Tough Conversations

- When conversations get tough, don't let the issue come between us and the other person. We need to work together to attack the issue.
- Don't count on other people changing. We can challenge them to grow, but they need to know that we accept them whether they change or not.
- Show respect for the other person even when we disagree. We can't let the issue destroy the relationship.

11

Skill #2—Eliminate Intimidation

A lion never loses sleep over the opinion of the
sheep.

African proverb

The taxi ride to the Minneapolis airport was a long one, because it was right in the middle of afternoon rush hour. But
I wasn't in a hurry. I had plenty of time before my flight. I was
tired, because I had just finished my fifth seminar in five days.
Talking for eight hours a day can be draining, especially for
an introvert. I had used up all my words for the week, so I was
hoping to relax and just stare out the window during the drive.

My driver had a different agenda. He was one of the chattier
drivers I've encountered over the years and was committed to
having a conversation. His thick Ugandan accent was tough
to understand, but he talked almost nonstop (often gestur-
ing with both hands off the steering wheel, which was a little

disconcerting). At first, I responded with short answers, hoping to buy just a few moments of quiet. But he missed my subtle hints and asked question after question.

I have to hand it to him; he did a good job making conversation. He seemed to follow the exact pattern I described in my book *How to Communicate with Confidence*—initiating, finding common ground, exploring, expanding, etc. Eventually, he asked, "What do you do?" I told him that I lead seminars in different corporations. He wanted to know the topics, details, and settings.

Finally, he found his hot button. "So let's say you stand in front of one hundred people to speak. They're at the same level as you, so they know as much as you do. How do you keep from being shy?"

"Shy?" I said.

"Yes, shy. You know—like when your hands shake and people see it and they don't like you."

I figured out that he was asking about feeling nervous and intimidated.

"I think everybody feels that way the first time they're in front of the group," I said. "The more you do it, the more confident you get."

We were pretty engaged in the conversation by then, so I figured I could have my quiet time when I got to the airport.

"So how do you get over that?" he asked. We talked about different options, because it seemed that he really wanted a solution.

As we approached the airport, he said, "Someone told me once that if you're nervous, you should look over everyone's head and not look in their eyes. That's how you keep from being shy."

"Well," I responded, "I've heard that a number of times, and other gimmicks just like it. But from experience, I'd have to disagree."

"But isn't it more scary to look right at them?"

"It seems that way," I said. "But I've found it does just the opposite. If I try to avoid looking at them, it reminds me of how intimidated I feel. It's like not wanting to open your eyes during a scary movie, because you're afraid you'll see something that terrifies you. But when you look directly in their eyes, you connect with them. You have one of those human moments when they become a real person instead of something scary. They feel more connected to you, and you're able to relax. If you're 'shy,' they usually don't notice. And if you've connected with them, they don't care."

"What if you're talking to the mayor of the city?" he said. "How do you keep from being shy with him?"

"Look him in the eye," I said. "He might be the mayor, but if you look him in the eye, he becomes a person."

How to Keep from Being Shy

When someone makes solid eye contact with us during a conversation, they project confidence. If they also have a stronger personality than we do, it's easy to feel intimidated. We compare ourselves to them and end up on the inferior side of the equation. Once that happens, it's hard to have healthy dialogue. We see them through the filter of "you're better than me," so the balance becomes unrealistic. We've given them a competitive edge.

Tough communication only works when there's honesty in the relationship, no matter who it is with. I'm not talking about not telling lies. I'm talking about keeping the integrity of the relationship. We need to see the other person as they really are, not as an image we've projected onto them.

If we compare ourselves with people's outsides, everybody is either above us or below us in some way. If I see myself as inferior to you, I'll be frustrated and lack confidence in those tough conversations. If I see you as inferior to me, I won't respect you. The only way to make a relationship work is to see each other as people of true value. The inside, not the outside, determines our worth.

My wife, Diane, and I went to an exhibit last weekend of human bodies that had been preserved chemically so they could be permanently observed. They were real bodies, but the skin was missing so you could see the actual muscles, organs, blood vessels, nerves, etc. It was fascinating to be able to get a close-up view of the inner workings of the human body.

There was no way to tell what those people looked like when they were alive. One might have been a little taller or had a broader skeletal system, but they were essentially identical.

I thought that was a good lesson about intimidation. We tend to be intimidated by what we see on the outside. But under the skin, we're all the same: human. We could look at a homeless person and the president of a country side by side and have totally different reactions. But inside, they're the same.

In my line of work, I encounter some pretty high-powered executives in major corporations and government agencies. There was a time when I was intimidated in those situations, because I figured they were in a different league. But with experience, I've discovered that they're just normal people who have achieved some great things and lead a lot of people. They might be taller, more experienced, richer, or more powerful than I am. But they put their pants on one leg at a time, just like I do. On the inside, they're human, just like me.

It doesn't matter if we're talking to a spouse, boss, child, family member, neighbor, politician, or executive. They might seem intimidating by their temperament or approach. But the common ground of humanness is where we connect without intimidation.

Why We Focus on the Negative

When I teach seminars, I have people fill out evaluation forms at the end of the session. They give their opinion about the content, the relevance, and the facilitator, rating those issues on a scale of 1 to 10. In talking to other people who facilitate regularly, we've discovered that we all approach those evaluations in the same way:

- We look at the score they give us (the facilitator) before the score they give the seminar (content).
- We can get fifty scores of 10 and one score of 4, and we're depressed about the 4.

We're more interested in what they think of us than what they think of the seminar, and we're upset if one person in the group doesn't like us.

If fifty people like a session and one doesn't, it's only logical to say that the one person is the issue. If one person likes a session and fifty don't, I have to admit that I'm the issue. (Someone said that if one person tells you you're a horse, just ignore them. If fifty people tell you you're a horse, look for a saddle.)

At first, I thought I was the only one who focused on the negative. But in training and mentoring facilitators over the years, I've discovered that this is common ground. Why is it so easy to focus on the negative and ignore the positive?

In the same way, why do single, negative experiences when we're growing up determine our lens for evaluating every relationship in the future? If someone told us as a child that we were irritating, we go through life trying to avoid being an irritation to others.

It turns out there are actually physiological reasons for this. Some of the most recent brain research has discovered that our brains are wired for negative stimuli more than positive stimuli. One researcher said that our brains are like Velcro for negative experiences but like Teflon for positive ones. We tend to overestimate how bad a danger is and underestimate how valuable a positive experience can be. We also tend to underestimate our abilities to deal with negative experiences as well as to take advantage of positive opportunities for growth and advancement. In other words, we think with a negative bias. We're more likely to be pessimistic than optimistic by nature.

There's a tiny part of the brain called the amygdala that's responsible for such things. When it picks up a negative experience, it sends that experience into long-term storage immediately. But we have to focus on a positive experience for about twelve seconds before it gets stored.

Our brains are wired to go after bad news and ignore good news. That's why we can be in the middle of ninety-nine good experiences but focus on the one bad thing that happens. We focus more on threats than opportunities. If we miss an opportunity, our brains tell us it's okay—another one might come along tomorrow. But if we feel a threat, our brains remind us that it could mean pain that might last a long time.

So how does this apply to relationships and tough conversations? There can be a lot of positive things happening in our relationships. But when something negative happens, we focus on it. We lose perspective because we concentrate on the one negative and ignore the dozens of positives.

We pass by a friend at church and say, "Hi." They make eye contact but don't respond or smile. We think, "Why didn't they respond?" We spend the rest of the day wondering what we did that upset them, and it ruins our day. But when we finally talk to them, we find out that they didn't even see us. They were lost in thought about something, and we didn't even register on their consciousness.

We pick up cues from other people and interpret them without ever checking to see if our perspective is accurate. From that point on, we believe our perspective is true, and it impacts our relationships with those people. All of this happens in our heads, and the other person doesn't have a clue!

When we get intimidated by another person, it's usually not because of what they say or do. It's because of how we interpret what they say or do. We assume the other person is feeling a certain way without finding out if it's true.

As an example, let's revisit our discussion about temperaments. Extroverts tend to be quick on their feet and speak their minds quickly. Introverts tend to think deeper but need time to process information before they express their thoughts.

In conflict, the extrovert might feel they've won the argument because the introvert couldn't come up with a good answer. The introvert feels intimidated because they can never hold their own in a tough conversation. "It's hopeless," they think. "I never know what to say, so I can't compete with them. Any time we talk through tough issues, I lose."

It goes back to perspective. Introverts assume that the other person is more confident because they speak their mind so quickly. But that ignores the facts about the differences in temperament:

- Extroverts develop their opinions by talking. They often decide what their position is during dialogue, not before. When they're talking, it might be the first time a particular idea has ever entered their mind. Since they're able to think quickly, they assume that everyone else can do the same. So when an introvert can't respond, the extrovert thinks they've won.

- Introverts develop their opinions by thinking. They take information in during a conversation but need time to

143

ponder and process what they've heard before they come up with opinions. They don't know what they think yet. When they can't respond quickly, they feel like they've lost the argument.

As we learned earlier, extroverts tend to think faster. Introverts tend to think deeper. Success comes when both sides recognize the reality of their temperaments instead of thinking the other person needs to change. Introverts need to understand that reality. When an extrovert shoots out quick, forceful arguments, this doesn't mean they're correct. It means they have a different style.

When an extrovert is talking, an introvert needs a realistic response to avoid intimidation. "Wow, you make some really good points. Right off the top of my head, I'm not sure how to respond. I need a little time to think this through. Let me play with your ideas for a day or two, and I'll get back with you. Maybe I'll shoot you an email with my reactions, or we can grab a cup of coffee. Then I'd love to hear what you think about my thoughts."

Writing and pondering give introverts a chance to think first and then respond well without intimidation. That's an introvert's strength, and they shouldn't be embarrassed about it. This approach gives both extroverts and introverts a chance to process in their own way.

What Are We Supposed to Do?

Knowing how our brains operate with a bias toward the negative, we need to be conscious about how we process perceived threats. We need to rewrite the warning on our right-hand-side car mirror: Objects in this mirror are smaller than they appear.

When we don't connect with the people in our lives, our minds make up stories about what they're thinking (and those stories are usually negative). When we believe those negative stories, we get intimidated.

Psychologist Daniel Amen refers to this process as ANTs: Automatic Negative Thoughts.[1] These are the thoughts that come into our minds automatically and ruin our day. He says that they should have taught us in second grade that we don't have to believe every thought that comes into our head, and we have the ability to challenge those thoughts.

He suggests that whenever we feel sad, mad, nervous, or out of control, we should do two things:

1. Write down the negative thoughts (which gets them out of our head).
2. Ask ourselves if they're true.

Amen says, "One way to learn how to change your thoughts is to notice them when they are negative and talk back to them. If you can correct negative thoughts, you take away their power over you. When you just think a negative thought without challenging it, your mind believes it and your body reacts to it."[2] We don't want to give someone else the keys to our sanity. Intimidation comes when we fail to question someone else's perception of us.

So anytime we feel intimidated by someone during a tough conversation, we might need to remind ourselves of what's true:

- Am I intimidated by what they say or by what I think they mean?
- They're not better or worse than me; they're human.
- If I'm focusing on the negative, I need to remind myself of the positive.
- I don't want to assume what they're thinking; I need to explore.

- Their communication style isn't better or worse than mine; it's just different.
- I don't have to compare and be like them; I need to be myself.

So how do we keep from being intimidated? By focusing on what's true instead of what we feel—choosing accuracy over perception. Doing so takes time and effort, but the return on this investment can be huge. This is a different way of thinking, but it can help us hold our own when a conversation gets tough.

Tips for Tough Conversations

How can we keep from feeling intimidated by others?

- Remember that we're all human. We all have fears and challenges but different styles of coping with them.
- Be intentional about focusing on positive perspectives instead of negative ones.
- Challenge the negative thoughts we have about ourselves to see if they're true.
- Realize that different temperaments communicate in different ways. They're not right or wrong; they're just different.

12

Skill #3—Practice Power Listening

> Most conversations are simply monologues delivered in the presence of a witness.
>
> Margaret Millar[1]

Everybody has a story.

You have one. I have one. And we want someone to listen to our story. So we try to tell it—but nobody's listening. They're busy telling their own story.

I'm writing this as I sit in seat 8B on a two-hour flight from Portland to Ontario, California. Sometimes on a plane, I read; sometimes I work. Tonight, I'm observing. I'm surrounded by people who are all doing different things. I'm wondering about their stories.

Right next to me is 8A, sound asleep. I can't even guess his story, because he's just leaning against the window. But I still wonder.

Just ahead, 7A is probably in her late eighties. Through thick, black-framed glasses, she's reading an article titled "Modern Techniques for Dating." She's been studying it for the past fifteen minutes. I'd love to know her story.

Behind me, across the aisle in 9C and 9D, are two sisters—probably in their late seventies. They are talking nonstop and totally amused with everything the other one says. I overhear their conversation:

"Why haven't we taken off yet?"
  "I don't know—let me look out the window."
"What do you see?"
  "Oh, there's another plane landing. I can see it way off in the distance. Or at least I see the lights."
"Then it must be a plane."
  "Or maybe it's a bird. Maybe it's a bird with lights."

And they start laughing so hard they snort. Then they laugh harder because they snorted.

We've been in the air for over an hour now. They're still laughing at the things each other says. I'd love to know their story. If I were close enough to ask them, they'd probably be laughing too hard to tell it.

Directly across the aisle—8C—a late-twenties mom, is entertaining her two-year-old. He's wearing a gray T-shirt, a red and white embroidered necktie, and a gray derby hat. Look up *cute* in the dictionary and his picture would probably be there. He's busy with his electronic Etch A Sketch and loving the time with his mom. He has a story. It's a short story, but it's a story.

The last woman to board sits in 7C. Another elderly woman, she's dressed in her traveling best. A red blazer, tan slacks, and gold jewelry complete the look, evidence that she was stylin' when she was younger. She has a story. And she's telling her story.

From the moment she sat down, she's been talking to 7D—a midthirties woman who has the window seat. It's a small plane (two seats on each side), so 7D is a captive audience. But 7D is listening. Actively listening.

I felt sorry for her at first, because 7C is telling her entire life story. She talked about her upbringing, her kids, her late husband, her career, and her journey as a teenager. She talked about where she lived and what she enjoyed throughout her life. 7D is asking questions, which prompts 7C to talk even more.

7C is talking nonstop. 7D is *listening* nonstop.

God bless 7D. She's giving 7C a gift—the gift of listening. 7C will go home tonight feeling valued because a stranger took the time to care. 7C did 90 percent of the talking, but she'll always remember what a good conversationalist 7D was.

As a practicing introvert, I don't go out of my way to talk to people on airplanes. Usually, I've been talking all day in a seminar, so I want to rest. I'm learning how much it means to people when someone listens to their story. All I have to do is set it in motion, set aside my own agenda, and listen—and enjoy hearing a good story.

I want to know why an almost-ninety-year-old woman is reading about dating. I want to know what makes someone laugh at nothing until they can barely breathe. I want to know the journey of a little, tiny Etch A Sketch artist. I want to listen . . . and I want someone to listen to me.

Why We Want Someone to Listen

It's frustrating when someone accuses us of something without hearing our side of the story. Our boss yells at us for coming in late, saying we should have had the decency to at least call and let them know. If they had asked what happened, we could have explained that we *did* call but their voice mailbox was full.

But when those tough conversations begin with accusations and assumptions, we find it hard to communicate well.

People are starved to be listened to. We have many conversations, but true listening doesn't happen very often. Constant conversation is like trying to survive on a junk food diet, while listening provides the balanced emotional nutrition that gives us life.

Here's how the process breaks down:

- We all have a need to feel valued.
- When people listen to us, we feel valued. When they don't listen, we feel like we don't matter.
- The need to feel valued is strong. If nobody is listening, we talk more, hoping to catch their attention so they'll listen.
- Everybody's doing the same thing, trying to get people to listen. So everybody's talking, and nobody's listening.

Over the years, we've developed a culture of talkers instead of listeners. We've developed a collective mind-set that giving advice is more valuable to people than listening to them. If we want to help someone, we just tell them what they should do. Sounds helpful, right? They have a problem, and we have a solution. It's a match made in heaven.

There's a problem. Advice almost never solves problems. Listening does. This sounds counterintuitive, but it's true in most cases. If someone gives advice, we don't feel like listening. But if they listen to us, we feel like seeking their advice.

Think about the last time somebody gave you advice—or used facts and figures to convince you that your position was wrong and theirs was right. You probably didn't say, "Wow! That's so much better than my perspective. It's obvious that my position is wrong, so I'll immediately change my thinking and do exactly what you suggest." No, you probably thought they were crazy or arrogant—and either argued with them or simply withdrew from the conversation.

That's why we're so hesitant to open the door when someone comes to sell us a magazine subscription, push their religion, or sell candy for a cause. The person at the door is there to convince. They might have practiced the right responses to make us think they're listening, but their true motives tend to leak out.

When we want people to listen to us, our natural tendency is to talk more. After all, when we talk, it gives them something to listen to, right? But the exact opposite is true. The best way to get someone's attention is to listen to them. People instinctively want to hear what someone has to say when that person has first expressed genuine interest in them.

So the key is to talk less, not more. The same letters make up the words *listen* and *silent*.

The Value of Silence

During my years as a college professor, students would often drop by my office to talk. Some had questions about assignments, while others were wondering about what courses to take the next semester.

Usually, those conversations morphed into life conversations. They were negotiating the real world away from their parents and trying to figure things out. They needed someone they trusted to bounce ideas around with.

I loved those conversations. They were one of the best parts of my job. I was also amazed at the impact those conversations had. Students would share their thoughts, their dreams, and their challenges. They would talk about . . . well, just *stuff*. I almost never had answers. I just had ears. I always felt inadequate, thinking I should have better advice—better things to say. I should have been able to draw deeply from my well of experience and wisdom, delivering pearls of insight that would blow them away. The well usually felt pretty dry.

So I just listened. Whenever possible, I would simply affirm something I had noticed about them that was an area of strength. Surprisingly, they often had no idea they had that strength. It simply never occurred to them. To me, it was a casual conversation. To them, it was a turning point.

People are starved to have someone listen to them. The act of listening tells them they have value when they don't value themselves. If they don't believe in themselves, they borrow our belief in them when we listen—until it becomes their own.

The more important a relationship is, the more valuable listening is. When two people in conflict keep talking "at" each other, they're pouring fuel on an open flame. But when those same two people learn to listen to each other, the fire runs out of fuel and cools down.

Learning to Listen

Listening is a skill that anyone can learn. It's not reserved for introverts or sensitive types. The noisiest of us can learn to listen if we're intentional. We need to recognize two things:

1. why we don't listen
2. how we can improve our listening

Why We Don't Listen

There are a number of common situations in which we find ourselves talking instead of listening:

- *We believe we're right.* If we're convinced of our position, it's easy for us to think the other person is ignorant or stubborn. We don't really want to hear their position because listening would be pointless.

- *We think the problem is the other person's fault.* If we believe the other person is to blame and we're absolutely blameless, we don't feel the need to explore our part in the issue. We simply want the other person to shape up.

- *We're afraid of criticism.* If we don't like conflict, we do whatever we can to avoid it. We present our position and get defensive when the other person talks, which effectively shuts down communication.

- *We feel like we deserve to be treated well.* If we interpret the other person's approach as criticism, we shut down. We feel like we're not being respected, so we're not open to hearing their perspective.

- *We're afraid we'll lose ground if we admit we're wrong.* If two people are trying to determine who is right and who is wrong instead of exploring the issue, the conversation stalls. If we admit we're wrong, we feel like we let the other person win.

- *We want to be in control.* We don't like being a passenger in a car with a crazy driver. They're behind the wheel, and we're afraid of what's going to happen. We'd much rather be in the driver's seat.

- *We think faster than they talk.* If someone takes their time forming their ideas, we want to finish their sentences for them to move the conversation along. We get bored and distracted, so we give up listening.

When we find ourselves not listening, that should be a trigger for us to analyze what's happening in the relationship. Becoming conscious of the underlying reason for our inattention is the first step in developing a solution.

How We Can Improve Our Listening

Most people develop a pattern of conversation that's quite ineffective:

- One person talks, but the other listens to prepare their reply.
- The second person gives their reply, and the first person is only thinking about how they'll respond next.
- The first person responds, and the other person listens so they know how to reply. . . .

And the pattern spirals downward into ineffectiveness. People are talking, but no one is listening.

To improve our listening, we need to shift our focus away from ourselves and genuinely focus on the other person. That doesn't mean we give up our needs and make the relationship all about them. It means we have regular periods when we temporarily set aside our agenda in order to look through their eyes. We're not listening so we can think up ways to counter their position; we're listening to simply see what they see. This can happen multiple times in a conversation. In fact, it becomes the pattern that is most effective for meaningful connection.

A healthy scenario is for one person to talk while the other person sets aside their own agenda and gives them 100 percent of their attention. When the conversation reverses, the same thing takes place.

"But what if they don't cooperate? I can listen to them, but what if they don't listen to me?"

That's a real possibility. We can't control what someone else does. We can only control the choices we make to stay focused, no matter what the other person does. Interestingly enough, if one person starts genuinely listening, that usually influences the other person.

Picture two people facing each other with both arms forward and pushing against each other's open palms. As long as they keep pushing, tension keeps them standing. But if one person backs off, the other won't have anything to push against and will fall forward if they keep pushing. It's awkward to keep pushing when the other person isn't pushing back. That's what happens during a tough conversation. If both people are just talking, it keeps the tension going and the struggle continues. But when one person starts to genuinely listen, it takes the pressure off. When that happens, it's tough for the other person to stay active in the conflict.

Proverbs says, "A gentle response defuses anger" (15:1). That sounds like a tough thing to do when we're feeling strong emotion. But learning to handle tough conversations effectively involves doing things differently than we normally do. It means we make intentional choices instead of just reacting to things people do or say. It goes back to our definition of insanity: doing the same thing we've always done and expecting different results.

If we want new results in our communication, we need to approach conversations in new ways. Those new approaches might include the following:

- *We listen first.* When a conversation turns challenging, it's easy to jump in with our opinion. It's better to switch our agenda from *convincing* to *understanding.* When we do that, we change the dynamics of the conversation.

- *We don't interrupt.* Good listeners don't jump in to finish another person's sentences when they take too long to form their thoughts. We can't be afraid of silence, and we show respect by not rushing them to a conclusion. We need to manage our own side of the conversation, not both sides.

- *We are aware of their responses.* When we're talking, it's easy to get caught up in our own thoughts and forget about the other person. Good listeners are always watching the subtle facial expressions and movements to see how the other person is responding.

- *We don't assume what they're thinking.* If there aren't any visual cues, it's easy to assume the other person is disagreeing with us. The only way to find out is to ask: "How are you responding to this? What are you thinking right now?"

- *We practice underexplaining.* During tough conversations, we have a tendency to overexplain an issue when the other person isn't agreeing. When that happens, we repeat ourselves and talk in circles, which frustrates the other person. It's better to state our position and then leave it up to them to ask for clarification.

- *We ask a question to keep momentum going.* If it seems like the other person isn't listening, we shouldn't talk more. Instead, we should quit talking and ask a question: "Am I making sense?" That turns the momentum back over to them to continue the conversation.

- *We ask clarifying questions for understanding.* Instead of reacting to everything they say, we slow down and ask clarifying questions to make sure we're on the same page. Clarifying questions dig deeper into an issue.

  "When you say that money is the problem, what does that look like?"

  "Could you tell me more about that?"

  "You say I don't pay attention to your needs. Could you be more specific?"

  "When you say you want better results from my work, what would better results look like to you?"

- *We talk about things they're interested in.* We'll have trouble complaining to a vegan about the rising cost of meat.

- *We summarize what they've said.* If we want the other person to know we were listening, we should summarize what they said in our own words and ask them if we've gotten it correct. "So if I'm hearing you correctly, you're thinking . . . Am I getting that right?"

Tips for Tough Conversations

Listening is one of the simplest ways to break down barriers during tough conversations. We need humility to practice it, but it is one of the fastest ways to connect honestly when a relationship is more important than an issue.

- Ask someone to tell their story. Then look them in the eyes while they talk.
- Give someone the gift of genuine listening. It's the fastest way to soften strain during a tough conversation.
- Practice listening with everyone. We need to set aside our own agenda and just listen to understand.
- Reply by clarifying what someone says rather than adding our own thoughts. Whenever we shift the focus to us, we're not listening anymore—we're talking.

13

Skill #4—Encourage Honest Feedback

I need someone that laughs at all my jokes. You know, honest feedback.

Mr. Burns, *The Simpsons*[1]

When I wrote my first book a few years ago, I assumed I was a great writer. I worked on the first chapter, honing it and polishing it until it was perfect. I started picturing sold-out book signings, rave reviews in newspapers, and people stopping me on the street for autographs. And of course I pictured Oprah's unending praise as she gave everyone in her audience a copy of my book instead of a car (and they were thrilled).

Then I showed that single chapter to my wife. "Could you read this and let me know what you think?" I watched her as she read at the kitchen counter, waiting for her to respond with quivering excitement or even a small tear trickling down her cheek. She didn't show any emotion, so I assumed she was waiting until she was finished to say, "This is the best thing that's ever been written. Where will we put your 'Book of the Year' award?"

Finally, she finished. She simply said, "I don't get it."

What? She didn't get it? I figured she must have misread something. So I said, "You don't get it? What do you mean?"

She responded, "I just don't get it. The middle part didn't make sense, and I'm having trouble putting it all together."

My first thought was that she needed to improve her reading skills. But I took the manuscript over to the corner of the living room and read it again in my fetal position. Armed with her feedback, I saw exactly what she meant.

Four books later, I've learned never to hit send on any chapter or article she hasn't looked at. I'm too close to be objective. She sees what I don't and helps me capture a different perspective that makes all the difference. It may not be comfortable, but I need honest feedback.

Expanding Our Perspective

Feedback is critical for handling tough conversations. When words get tense with a spouse or teenager, it's easy to tell them our perspective before asking for their perspective. If we believe our perspective is accurate, we block effective communication.

We all think we're right on most things. After all, if we thought we were wrong, we would have changed our minds. So when someone sees something differently than we do, we assume they're either inaccurate or stubborn.

One day when I was in high school, I was standing with friends at an intersection when an accident occurred right in front of us. The police came and interviewed us individually, and we told them exactly what we saw happen.

Soon, an older woman across the street started yelling to the officers. "Hey! Come talk to me! I saw the whole thing!" We didn't remember her being there before, so we followed the police across the street and listened to her side of the story. It was totally different from what we had seen.

"Why is she lying?" we asked each other. "That's not what happened at all! What's she trying to pull?"

But then someone told us to turn around and look at the wreckage. From that perspective, her story made perfect sense.

I realized at that point that no matter how right I think I am, there's always another perspective. A conversation is not a matter of deciding who is right and who is wrong. In most cases, it involves listening carefully to both perspectives to see what the truth of the situation really is. King Solomon wrote, "The first to plead his case seems right, until another comes and examines him" (Prov. 18:17 NASB).

During a tough conversation, people often fight it out to decide who is correct. But if both people are doing the same thing, they are going to have a tough time reaching the truth. Pride gets in the way of the relationship.

It takes humility during a tough conversation to listen to another person's perspective. But it's the only way to make progress. We shouldn't try to *defend* our position as much as try to *complete* it.

We Need a Mirror

When someone points out that we have broccoli between our teeth, we're embarrassed. We instantly think of all the people who must have seen it but didn't say anything. That makes the situation even worse. It's painful to hear the truth, but we want to hear it so we can fix whatever is wrong.

Ken Blanchard, author of *The One-Minute Manager*, says, "Feedback is the breakfast of champions."[2] If we want to grow, we need honest feedback. If we want our relationships to grow, we need to get accurate feedback—and learn how to give it as well.

Giving up our need to be right all the time is risky. If we open our mind to explore another person's side of things, we're admitting that we might not have the whole picture. That's a tough thing to admit if our goal is to win the argument. It's even tougher if we're willing to explore and the other person isn't, because we're afraid they'll see it as a sign of weakness and pounce on it.

I have a friend who asks me for professional input on a regular basis. She often has controversy with her employer and feels that the organization is taking advantage of her. Usually, she builds a strong case of why she's justified in her feelings and why her employer is wrong. Generally, she's accurate. Her concerns are real and justified.

But she has the wisdom and openness to bounce her concerns off me before she goes to her employer, just to see if there's something she's missing. I'm not smarter than she is; I'm just a little further along on the corporate road than she is. So I've encountered some of the potholes she's just now experiencing. I'm on the outside, so I can see elements of truth in both perspectives. I don't have to take sides. I can show her things that might be valid from her employer's point of view and hold up a mirror so she can see how her approach might come across. Getting feedback doesn't make her right or wrong; it makes her *accurate*.

Known versus Unknown

If we're going to be honest with ourselves, we need to see ourselves as clearly as possible. Years ago, Joseph Luft and

Harrington Ingham developed a diagram called the Johari Window[3] to help people understand the relationships with themselves as well as with others. It's a simple tool that helps us see ourselves honestly so we can grow.

There are four areas of awareness:

1. *Open*. There are things I recognize about myself that you also know. This includes the things we've talked about or are obvious, such as my having a friendly disposition or a stubborn streak. If I accidently fall into a swimming pool at a party, the incident is hard to keep hidden. I know I fell in; you know I fell in (and you've already posted a video on social media).

2. *Blind*. This is the broccoli between my teeth. You know about it, but I don't. I'm blind to it. The only way I'll find out is if I happen to walk by a mirror or you tell me.

3. *Hidden*. These are the things I know about myself but haven't told you—my deep, dark secrets that I don't tell anyone, like the fact that I appear confident but really feel insecure inside. I'm embarrassed about these things and want to hide them, thinking you won't like me as much if you find out.

4. *Unknown*. There are a lot of things I don't know about myself, and you don't know them either. As I grow and mature over the years, I discover more and more of them. They typically surface when I'm in a safe relationship with someone and we're exploring together. They also include those deep-seated hurts that explain why I respond the way I do when I'm under pressure, even though I don't know they're there. In those cases, they might be discovered only through the efforts of a skilled therapist.

The *open* areas typically emerge in the initial stages of a relationship. There are obvious things about the other person that we identify with, and they connect with us in the same way:

- A couple finds areas of common interest and attraction.
- An employer sees skills in a prospective employee that would add value to the team.
- A new neighbor's care of their yard (or lack of care) becomes an obvious area of mutual interest.

Where it gets interesting is when the *blind* and *hidden* areas begin to surface. The more we get to know another person, the more we find out about them. When a couple has their first fight, it's usually because something unexpected showed up. We point out something about the other person that they didn't notice, or they tell us something about us that we didn't know. This throws off the equilibrium in the relationship and causes us to reevaluate what we believed was true.

Sometimes in conflict, emotions surface where there's no explanation for them. This makes conversations tough, because logic doesn't resolve the issue. In those cases, we're often looking at the *unknown* areas. They're under the surface, so they're not obvious. Trying to solve the problem becomes futile, because we're ignoring a deeper issue.

If both people involved in a tough conversation have the same perspective, there wouldn't be a disagreement. When there is disagreement, the obvious need is to cross the street and see what the other person is seeing.

Then what's the problem?

1. The other person might not be willing to come to our side of the street.
2. We can't force them to change.
3. We can only change ourselves.

In an earlier chapter, we compared conversation to a game of checkers. If we get overly focused on how poorly the other person is playing, we're not making the game any better. We need to stay on our side of the board and work on our game.

Getting to the Truth

How do we work on our own game? How do we build our own skills for tough conversations no matter how others respond? We need feedback from people we trust. We need to find out the blind areas that are getting in the way of effective connection with others. We need to find the broccoli between our teeth.

It's tough to get accurate feedback from people. While a few people might feel like it's their job to point out our faults, most people are sensitive enough to avoid hurting our feelings. They don't volunteer feedback because they don't want to become a critic. The only way we'll get accurate feedback from others is by taking the initiative to get it and to make it safe for the right people to give it.

The process involves three steps:

1. asking for feedback
2. receiving feedback
3. responding to feedback

Asking for Feedback

If we could videotape ourselves 24/7, we'd get an accurate picture of how we come across to others. Since that's not possible, we need to hear from people we trust. Usually the people we don't trust as much give us their unsolicited opinion, while the people we trust are hesitant to provide it. Caring friends are the only ones who can give caring feedback.

That means we have to ask for it. If we don't ask, we won't get it. We also should ask for *specific* feedback. It's tough for someone to respond to a question like, "Do you think I'm a jerk?" It's safer for them if we phrase things carefully:

- "I really want to know how I come across to others. Could you think about it for a few days and let me know one thing I could work on to be a better friend?"
- "If somebody asked you what my greatest strength was, what would you say?"
- "Is there anything I do during conversations that keeps me from being a good listener?"

The more specific the question, the easier it is for people to give valuable feedback. If we just say, "So what do you really think of me?" we'll probably get a generic response like, "You're fine." (That's better than saying, "You need to be taller.")

Receiving Feedback

We need to make it comfortable for people to give us feedback, because they're taking a risk in doing so. Some people will give us verbal feedback over coffee, while others need time to process and put their thoughts in an email. I've found that taking a walk with someone enables them to share their thoughts without having to look me in the eyes.

When we receive feedback, we need to listen, not defend. We're asking for their perspective, where they hold up a mirror for us. If we start giving explanations for our actions when they tell us things they see, they'll stop telling us.

A great way to show that we value their input is to take notes while they talk. This says, "Your opinion is really important to me, so I want to make sure I capture it."

Responding to Feedback

Even if we received feedback from a close friend, we should send them a note a couple of days later thanking them for the feedback. We should let them know how much it meant that they took the risk to be honest with us and how much we value their relationship.

A few weeks later, we could let them know something we've done to act on their feedback and how it has impacted an important relationship we have. If nothing changes, they probably won't give us feedback in the future. But if we take action on it, they recognize that we value their perspective and will be much more open to providing feedback in the future.

Even healthy relationships encounter tough conversations. When they occur, they should lead us on a journey to discover truth. Humility becomes the fertile ground for a relationship to grow.

When It Goes Both Ways

Yes, we can only change ourselves. But as our conversational skills grow, others might become more open to receiving feedback from us. How do we give feedback? By keeping it personal—giving our perspective as another view, not as absolute truth.

Many books talk about using "I messages" instead of "you messages" during tough conversations. This might feel trite and overused, but it's still important.

"You messages" put people on the defensive. When we say, "You always . . . You never . . . It's your fault . . . You need to . . . Why can't you . . ." people feel like they're being attacked.

"I messages" can be honest, because we're not telling the other person they're wrong. We're just giving our perspective. Instead of saying, "You frustrate me!" we could say, "When you say that, I feel frustrated." We're giving our perspective instead of telling them they're wrong.

In tough conversations, making accusations and demeaning the other person always takes us away from the real issues. We want to hurt them because they're hurting us. We want to attack and punish. If that's not appropriate (maybe because we work for them), we withdraw, become passive-aggressive, or bad-mouth them behind their back. Such actions always make the problem worse, not better. They're a form of relational road rage.

The solution? We need to own our side of the conversation, giving our perspective without making judgments about their character or actions. We can't control what another person does or feels, but we can control how we respond to them. We need to see each other's perspective in order to discover truth rather than fighting to see who's right. As the cliché says, "There are two sides to every situation." If we explore them, we make a major move toward healing and solutions.

Conversational success comes through truth, not triumph.

Tips for Tough Conversations

How can we get the feedback we need?

- Ask for it.
- Make it safe for others to share feedback.
- Listen to their input without becoming defensive.
- Remember that their input is their perspective, not necessarily full truth. We have to decide how we'll respond to it.

14

Skill #5—Start with Kindness

Kindness is the language which the deaf can hear
and the blind can see.

Mark Twain[1]

"Do you want to get to the end of your life and have people
just say, 'He was *nice*'?" the speaker asked. "Is that what
you want on your tombstone? No!" he continued. "You want
to make a difference! You need to be strong and confident! You
want to be forceful about making change! You don't want to
just be *nice*!"

I was probably about ten years old at the time. I don't remember the setting or who the speaker was. I only remember
his words. And I remember thinking, *What's so bad about being
nice?*

Even at that young age, I had met a lot of forceful, confident
people. I admired them, but I wasn't drawn to them. The people

I looked up to the most were nice. I looked forward to being around them. They made me feel safe.

I would watch the forceful people and think, "I wish I could be forceful and confident like them." It seemed like most people admired those strong personalities and looked down on the quiet ones. I wasn't one of those forceful personalities and figured that I needed to become that way if I ever wanted to make a difference. But my efforts were futile. I felt like a parakeet trying to turn into a panther.

Is It Enough to Just Be Nice?

Over the years, I've thought about the people who have had the greatest impact on my life. Some were forceful, and others were not. I've had some tough encounters with people who forcibly put me in my place, and I changed because of it. I usually prefer the gentle approach because it's more comfortable. It just feels better when people are nice to you. But those strong personalities definitely were appropriate when I needed a course change.

I've always assumed that it's best to be nice whenever possible. But when tough conversations take place and direct challenge is necessary, which is better—nice or tough? Can we be both?

I struggled with that paradox for a long time. I did some research to find out where niceness fits into our lives. I concluded that when it comes to those challenging times in important relationships, nice makes a good default setting. But it doesn't go far enough.

We need to move from nice to kind. Kindness usually involves being nice but goes much further. Being kind involves a gentle strength that comes from a base of confidence. People who are kind care deeply for others and are willing to do what's best for them in a way that values them.

Someone said that kind people say tough things in a nice way, while nice people never say anything tough. Nice people don't help others get better because they're focused on how they're perceived. Kind people help others get better because they're not dependent on them for their own value. Having a foundation of strength allows them to genuinely contribute to the lives of others.

I once asked the pastor of a large congregation, "What's the hardest thing you've ever had to do in all your years of ministry?" His answer was immediate: "I had to fire a volunteer."

As we talked, he described the fine line he had to walk when someone had become a liability but still needed to feel valued and cared about. "Nice" would have overlooked the issue, and it would have gotten worse. "Kind" meant the pastor had to make the tough decision because it was the best choice for both the person and the program.

The Downside to Being Nice

Last year I had surgery for a hernia. After several weeks of recovery, I was still experiencing some severe pain. Concerned, I made an appointment with the surgeon to find out what was happening. He was a very nice man, and I had appreciated his bedside manner during our earlier appointments.

When I questioned him about the consistent pain, I expected a calm, kind response. But instead, he almost shouted, "It hurts? Well, *of course* it hurts! I knocked you out and cut you with a knife. You think that's not going to hurt? And you paid me a lot of money to do it!" The slight smile and the twinkle in his eyes let me know he was serious but compassionate. He was still nice, but he was also kind. He didn't sugarcoat the healing that would have to take place.

The same thing is true in conversation. When we genuinely care about someone, there are times when we need to tell them the truth, even if it causes pain. It's wrong if we do it to relieve our frustration. But it's caring to do it because the person needs to recognize the impact their choices are having. It's the kind approach.

While niceness is a great characteristic to have, there's a problem when it exists in isolation. Niceness alone usually comes from a place of need, not a place of strength. When we don't have a strong sense of our own value, we depend on validation from other people. We need people to like us. Our self-worth and happiness depend on how other people feel about us—so we become nice so people will like us.

Nice people tend to avoid conflict. If there's conflict, people might not agree with us, which means they might be upset with us. We can't risk that, because our self-esteem is based on people liking us. So we try not to express negative emotions, even if we're feeling those emotions strongly. If we're angry or frustrated, we keep smiling. We don't want to offend anyone, so we keep our emotions stuffed inside.

That's a problem, because stuffed emotions tend to leak out over time. People might not notice at first. But over time, they start picking up the subtle clues that signal an emotional disconnect. Often, we begin by using uncharacteristic sarcasm in response to others. Sarcasm can be biting but has a certain degree of social acceptability because it's seen as witty or clever. But then we may turn to more passive-aggressive responses in which there's a sharp edge to our comments. We look people in the eyes and smile while we're feeling negative toward them, hiding our real feelings.

In our closest relationships, it's harder to hide because people know us well. Our words might sound okay, but they sense that our eyes aren't right, our smile isn't quite the same, or there's just something missing.

Imagine a two-liter bottle that's empty. Each emotion we feel is like a drop of water that we put inside the bottle. We're irritated—a drop goes in. We're angry—a drop goes in. We're frustrated—a drop goes in. Nobody notices the emotions because we've tucked them away in the bottle.

When the rough stuff of life happens, it's like smacking the bottle on the side. Things get shaken up and sloshed around, but the emotions are all inside and nobody notices. They think we just handle rough times well.

We can do that for a long time, and we get really good at keeping the emotions in the bottle. But over time, the bottle starts to fill up. When the level gets near the top and the bottle gets smacked, it's harder to keep everything inside. A few drops splash out the top, and people think, "What was that? That was different."

When the bottle is full, it simply can't hold any more emotions. So when life smacks the bottle, water gushes out the top. We have an emotional outburst because we just can't keep our emotions in anymore. Everybody gets wet, and there's a cleanup required in aisle 3. People are surprised at the outburst and wonder why we suddenly changed.

Nice people put a lot of energy into keeping things in the bottle. But this is an inward focus; everything is about making sure our image is protected. It's a lot easier to keep the drops out of the bottle in the first place.

I remember reading a book as a teenager that said it was bad to be angry. Somehow, that stuck with me. I spent the next few decades telling people that things didn't ruffle me much and that I was pretty laid-back. I convinced myself that I really didn't get angry and tried to convince others of the same thing. Two things happened:

1. I didn't have many close friends because I wasn't real with people (or myself).
2. I was surprised when the water started sloshing out of the bottle.

Over time, I realized that bottling up my emotions didn't make them go away; it pressurized them so that they exploded later on. It took me years to realize that I couldn't have close relationships or healthy conversations if I was just protecting my image.

Growing Up into Kindness

Many people have grown up trying to be pleasant and nice. But as the years pass, they feel disconnected from others because they haven't been real with others, which is the foundation for healthy relationships.

Conflict happens in the healthiest relationships. When nice people find themselves in conflict, they tend to shift the focus away from themselves.

- They withdraw to avoid the conflict.
- They minimize the issue.
- They use humor to deflect negative feelings.
- They try to change the subject.
- They focus on the other person's behavior to take the focus off themselves.

All of those strategies keep genuine, healthy communication from taking place. These people are focused on being the nice person, protecting themselves instead of dealing with the real issue. It's more important for them to be liked than to be genuine. They need to make the transition from niceness to kindness.

- Niceness alone comes from neediness. Kindness comes from confidence.
- Niceness alone feeds off being liked by others. Kindness simply cares about others no matter what they do.

- Niceness alone gives in to avoid conflict. Kindness sets boundaries when needed.
- Niceness alone operates from fear. Kindness operates from love and caring.
- Niceness alone is weak. Kindness is strong.
- Niceness alone is selfish. Kindness is selfless.
- Niceness alone lies to make itself feel better. Kindness speaks the truth in love.
- Niceness alone focuses inward to be perceived as nice. Kindness focuses outward.
- Niceness alone cares only about what others think. Kindness just cares.

Just to be clear: being nice isn't a bad thing unless it's the *only* thing. When the goal of being nice is to treat people with respect, it's a good thing. When the goal is to manipulate people into seeing us a certain way, it's a bad thing.

In tough conversations, niceness goes a long way. In tough conversations, niceness is often used to keep the other person from getting upset. That's okay if we want to keep the conversation civil and respectful. It's not okay if we keep our emotions bottled up. Emotions fuel our energy to find a solution. No emotion, no solution.

The real power in conversation comes when niceness has grown into kindness. We care deeply enough to tell the tough truth with gentleness and genuine respect.

Social Lubrication

Someone said that kindness is a social lubricant that greases the inner workings of any relationship.

It doesn't matter if our car is a Volkswagen or a Lamborghini; it needs to have the oil changed on a regular basis. If we ignore regular lubrication, the gears begin to grind and wear. In fact, most mechanics say that the most important thing we can do to extend the life of a car is to change the oil and lubricate the car on a regular basis.

The same thing is true of relationships. It doesn't matter if the relationship is three weeks old or thirty years old; it needs regular maintenance and lubrication. If we skip the lubrication, the gears begin to grind. Emotions and irritation become consistent companions, tempers flare, and conversations become tense. That's because we've taken the relationship for granted and ignored the routine maintenance. We're so focused on issues and feelings that we forget about kindness. Over time, we get irritated with the relationship and feel like it's time to trade it in for a new model.

Maybe it's just time for a little kindness.

The issues are real. The emotions are real. The conflict is real. But the need for lubrication is real as well. If we ignore it, we short-circuit the connection process. Any movement in the relationship will produce friction, and the best way to deal with friction is with lubrication.

A few months ago, our garage door started making noise when it opened or closed. This wasn't just a little noise; it was serious squeaking, shrieking, grinding, and rattling. It was an old door with an old electric opener, so I assumed it was finally falling apart. The noise could be heard throughout the house every time we used it, and I was afraid it would collapse on top of our cars.

We started pricing new garage doors and were stunned at how much it would cost to replace our current one. We knew we had to do something, because we knew it was only a matter of time before the door stopped working.

I was talking with a friend about it who asked, "Have you oiled the chain lately?" Well, of course I hadn't done that. The door had worked well for years without lubrication, so why would it need it now?

(You already know where this is going, right?) I went to Home Depot and purchased a tiny tube of garage door chain lubricant for a couple of dollars and squirted a few drops along the chain. I pushed the button. It was like we had a new garage door. No noise, no rattles, smooth operation. All because of a few drops of lubricant.

The song says, "Try a little kindness." It's amazing how far a little kindness goes in a relationship and how simple it is to apply. It's also amazing how we tend to ignore such a simple solution because it seems so insignificant in contrast to the issues we're working through.

Kindness is not a cure-all for every relationship problem; it will not eliminate conflicts and solve all our problems. But it will make it possible to deal with those issues in a way that keeps the relationship strong in the process. Kindness is a recurring reminder to the other person that we care about them. It gives the message that we're committed to them, we value them, and we think they're worth the effort to tackle tough issues together. It says, "This problem is big, but I think we're bigger."

The Mechanics of Kindness

"But what if I'm trying to be kind and the other person isn't? Doesn't that set me up to have them walk over me?" Three thoughts apply here.

First, that's more of a risk with niceness than with kindness. If we're trying to be nice so the other person will like us, we probably will get run over. We're coming from a position of weakness rather than strength. We're more concerned about how they perceive us than about the real issue.

Second, kindness isn't dependent on how somebody else responds. It's something we do because it's part of our character, not a technique to get the other person to be kind in return (though it often softens their approach). Kindness is a choice made by kind people. It's a strong position that allows us to treat others with respect regardless of the response.

Third, we can't change other people. We can influence them, but there's no guarantee they'll respond in a certain way. We don't use kindness to manipulate others so they'll come around. Too often we feel the need to fix others, and we're frustrated if they don't change. Relationships become a lot easier when we let go of our expectations of others and focus on what we can do. We can't control what others choose to do, but we can control what we choose to do.

Sometimes the other person is nice but not kind. They won't engage in meaningful dialogue or express honest emotions because they want us to feel good about them. What happens then?

We treat them with kindness. We tell the truth, make them feel safe, treat them with respect, and set boundaries. We encourage them to share their thoughts, and we don't get defensive when they do or try to explain their ideas away. We listen. We recognize that they may have experienced painful things in their past that caused them to adopt these coping strategies (abuse victims are often nice), and we give them space to grow.

Tips for Tough Conversations

In tough conversations, here are some ways to demonstrate kindness:

- *Take a kindness break.* Ask for a five-minute recess in which we affirm something about the other person or encourage them in some way.
- *Remind them of our commitment to the relationship.* Say, "This is really tough stuff, and it feels like we're in the

white-water rapids. You just need to be reminded that I'm not going anywhere. It's rough, but I'm staying in the boat."

- *If we walk away, always tell them when we're coming back.* Sometimes emotions get high, and we're too frustrated to keep talking. It's common for someone to say, "I just can't do this!" and walk away. There might be value in pulling away to let emotions settle, but we should always indicate that we'll return. "Give me a half hour. I just need some space, but I'll be back. Promise."

- *Don't take our case to others.* When we're frustrated with someone, it's easy to tell our side of the story to close friends to get their support. But that's unfair if they don't also get to hear the other person's side. We can be honest with close friends about the tough conversations we're having with someone, but we shouldn't get into the details in order to reinforce our position (or to have them take sides with us).

- *Tell them how much we value them, even when we don't agree with them.* Say, "I'm not sure I can go along with your thinking, but that doesn't change the fact that I value you simply for being you. Don't forget that. I'd love to explore your position more to see if I can understand."

- *Ask for what we need.* We shouldn't make people guess what we need; we should share it openly: "I just need you to listen." "I need some time to think before I respond." "I need you not to give up." Doing so will encourage them to do the same.

Everybody is going through something tough. Sometimes it involves us, sometimes it doesn't. If we're nice, we won't irritate them—but we won't help them either.

Kindness is the strength that builds relationships worth having.

15

Skill #6—Know Your Purpose

> There are only three kinds of people: those who
> let it happen, those who make it happen, and those
> who wonder what happened.
>
> Anonymous

When people graduate from high school, a long-standing tradition is to take a road trip. Friends get in a car and start driving, with no plans, no destination in mind, and no worries. The trip is symbolic of freedom, something they feel they've never had before.

Up until now, they've probably lived at home, having to follow rules their parents gave them. They've been in school, where they had to follow a rigid schedule and had consequences imposed on them if they didn't do their assignments on time. After graduation, they have a chance to test their wings. They've been itching to grow up, and this is their chance to toss the shackles and be free.

A road trip is usually a memorable experience, especially if done with friends. They experience the thrill of the open road and an open schedule. They see things they've never seen and get to decide where to go and what to do without anyone directing them.

Driving without a purpose might work for a road trip. But it doesn't work in relationships. Adult relationships are about connecting, communicating, and working together on something greater than ourselves. When two people have a common purpose, they have a teamwork that helps each of them grow. Without that mutual purpose, we can sabotage the future of the relationship.

Our Relational GPS

I recently had a conversation with a career pilot for a commercial airline. At least once a week, he makes a transatlantic flight to Paris, France. I asked the question I had always wondered: "That's a really long flight. What, exactly, do you do in the cockpit for all those hours to make sure you make it to Paris?"

"Really?" he said.

"Yes—in nontechnical terms."

"Okay," he responded. "Here's the simplest way I can describe what we do. First, we take off. Then we aim the plane toward Paris. Then we land."

"That's it?" I asked.

"Well, sort of," he said. "Once we take off, we encounter wind—and it blows us off course. So we have to re-aim for Paris. Then wind comes from a different direction, so we have to aim for Paris again. The wind and other forces are constantly taking us off course. So every few minutes, we have to aim for Paris again. It's all about aiming for Paris. Every decision we make is based on going to Paris. Otherwise, we might end up somewhere else without knowing how we got there."

We do the same thing in our cars when we use our GPS. We put in the address of our destination and start driving. From that point on, the GPS tells us where to turn, how far away the next turn is, and when we should arrive. If we turn the wrong way, the GPS recalculates a new route for us to get us back on track to our destination. If we don't put an address in, a GPS provides a really nice map that shows us exactly where we are.

We often meet people when our paths cross on the same map. We hang out together and might decide to travel together. The relationship might be:

- a romantic relationship
- a developing friendship
- a business partnership
- a neighborly connection
- a church or volunteer relationship

We get to know each other. We discover each other's likes and dislikes, unique habits (good and bad), and passions. We begin to see each other as we really are. If the relationship continues, we begin to look ahead. A couple asks, "Where is this relationship going?" Business partners ask, "What do we want to accomplish if this business goes forward?" New neighbors discuss, "Should we have both our houses painted and split the cost to save money?"

As relationships mature, they need to have a sense of purpose. For example, we don't just marry someone because we like them; we see the potential for a rewarding and meaningful life together. To keep the energy in the relationship, we need to know where we're headed.

We need to decide where Paris is and how we're going to get there. We need to focus on what's so special about Paris that it became our destination of choice. We need to put the address in our relationship GPS.

Why a Destination Is Important

A compelling destination gives us a reason to hang in there when conversations get tough. The more compelling the destination, the more power it has to keep us moving forward.

Several years ago, my wife and I were going to Hawaii. It was an award trip from the company I work for, and they would be covering all the expenses: airfare, meals, excursions, and lodging at one of the most elegant resorts on the island of Maui. It was a trip we never would have been able to afford ourselves, and it was going to provide a much-needed break from our crazy schedule of the past few months.

The weekend before the trip, we babysat our grandchildren. We knew they had the sniffles but didn't realize how potent their little germs were. We almost never get sick; when we do, we just power through it. But this time we were in bed the entire day before the trip, barely able to move. We couldn't imagine being able to make the trip.

But we also couldn't imagine missing the trip. When the alarm went off at 4:30 a.m., we felt a little better but had to make a quick decision. We were pretty sure we weren't contagious because the sickness had every characteristic of a twenty-four-hour flu. We felt miserable, but we figured it would be better to spend a week recovering in Hawaii than at home.

So we made the trip. The excitement of the experience was too good to pass up, and it gave us the ability to fight through the sickness.

That's what happens in relationships too. When we're moving together in an exciting direction toward a shared purpose, we have the energy to work through the toughest conversations along the way. We're not nearly as inclined to give up because we don't want to miss the outcome.

The toughest part is the middle of the journey. The beginning of any endeavor is exciting, and the culmination is energizing. But when we're in the middle of the process, plodding along through the mundane daily challenges, we can lose focus. We're like a marathon runner who hits "the wall" and feels they can't go on. The feeling of completion and the promise of the victory medal keep them going.

Seeing the "finish line" in a relationship gives us the energy to keep going when the conversations get tough. We work toward solutions and make things happen.

Course Corrections

Ideally, we determine the purpose of a relationship in the early stages of the relationship and then revisit it frequently. At the beginning of the journey, we are filled with excitement. It's easy to dream when we're not bogged down by the routines of life.

But it's not impossible to recalibrate in the middle of the journey, after the relationship has already hit some bumps. When tough conversations seem to be barriers to moving forward, we can hit the pause button and regroup. That's when we call a time-out from swatting flies to talk about patching the hole in the screen door.

Here's how this regrouping might look in several relationships.

Marriage. No one stands at the altar on their wedding day thinking, "Well, this won't last long." We have great hopes for the future and are committed to meeting the needs of the other person. We're energized by being together and want to build the relationship.

As time moves forward, life gets in the way. Job pressures increase, kids mysteriously appear and suck our energy away, and we just get tired. The initial excitement of the relationship wears thin, and we don't focus as much as we did before on meeting the needs of the other person.

Employment. A new job is exciting at the beginning, and we have high hopes for the partnership. The future looks bright, and there's hope for genuine growth and contribution.

But we find that the promises made by the company initially look different over time. We work to stay committed to the company, but our boss doesn't seem as committed to us. The newness wears off, and more is expected of us over time. We work longer hours and feel no one appreciates the effort we put in. The only time we get attention is when we do something wrong.

Neighbors. It's our dream house, and the neighborhood seems perfect. The schools have high ratings, and the kids have plenty of opportunities for sports and music. We meet the neighbors, who seem friendly enough.

But after a few weeks, the kids aren't connecting as well in school. The teacher turns out to be quite negative in her style, and we find out she barely made it through a probationary period last year after numerous complaints. One of the neighbors starts making subtle comments about the way we maintain our yard, and another one tends to show up at the door unannounced to talk several times a week. The soccer team is packed with demanding parents, and the music teacher won't respond to requests to discuss our child's progress.

Professionals. New insurance means a new family doctor. He's the one assigned to us, and we make appointments for our annual physicals. The first few appointments go well, and he seems to be competent enough.

But when more serious issues arise, we begin to question his skill. He seems to rush through the examinations, then determine a solution quickly. We feel he's not as thorough as he was in the past and are concerned he's simply writing prescriptions without a careful diagnosis. We try to ask questions, but he doesn't listen—and rushes to the next patient.

In all of these situations, we have high expectations when the relationships start well. But over time, the relationships aren't as fulfilling as they once were. We hit a time in the desert with no oasis in sight. We run dry.

During those desert times, we need to recalibrate the relationship. Having a clear purpose helps us make those midcourse corrections. When things get tough, we can stop and remind each other what our ultimate goal is (which usually is the health of the relationship). Then we evaluate each tough issue in light of the purpose of the relationship. Having a clear purpose becomes a personal constitution by which we can make tough decisions. Without that purpose, there's no criteria to use in judging our potential choices.

It's All about People

Benjamin Franklin said, "If you fail to plan, you are planning to fail."[1] That applies in every area of life, including our relationships. The more important something is, the more important planning becomes. We wouldn't build a house without a blueprint or pursue a college degree without a personalized schedule. Why wouldn't we spend time planning the direction of our most important relationships?

In my corporate consulting work, I've been teaching people how to manage projects for over two decades. I've been to classes on project management, read books, and studied articles. Most of these people use specific, detailed charts and diagrams to manage and fine-tune every detail of a project. Logic would tell us that if we can keep our fingers on all the details found in those charts, the project will succeed.

But most people have found that projects don't fail because of missing details. Projects fail because of *people*:

- unclear expectations
- conflicting priorities
- differing perspectives
- changing emotions
- limited time
- differing communication styles

When effective project managers begin a project, they don't say, "Why bother? The people aren't going to get along, and their differences will keep us from succeeding. We might as well not start. It's not worth it."

Project managers construct a plan. They make sure they have a worthy objective, that the motivation is clearly communicated to team members, and that they put the necessary energy into the people side of things.

Harold Kerzner estimates that a project manager spends 90 percent of their time communicating.[2] So the best charts and diagrams are worthless if the communication isn't dealt with. Most project management classes skim over the people issues that sabotage projects. But that's exactly where the focus needs to be to ensure that projects are completed successfully.

Flying to Paris involves a flight plan, but it takes into account the reality of the winds that can push the plane off course. A fulfilling relationship can have a solid plan, but we also have to take into account the real-life events that threaten to keep us from achieving our goal—and they're usually people issues.

The Process of Getting to Paris

How do we stick to the purpose of a relationship? These five steps keep us on track:

1. Get clear on the reason for the journey.
2. Be intentional.
3. Plan backward.
4. Schedule check-in sessions.
5. Act daily.

Get Clear on the Reason for the Journey

Knowing the purpose of a relationship provides a tool for managing tough conversations. Once the purpose is in place, it's easier to stop a volatile conversation and say, "Why are we having this conversation?" We'll be able to see if it's leading to our destination or if we're just attacking each other to get rid of our emotions. The emotions might still be there, but having a shared destination encourages people to fight fair as they head in the same direction.

Long-term purpose answers the question, "Where is this relationship headed?" It's a logical question to ask early in a relationship but a priceless one to ask after thirty years.

A couple wants to landscape the yard of their new home. He wants a pool, and she wants a garden—but there's not enough room for both. When they explore their motivations, the pool and the garden aren't the issues. He wants to have friends come over and hang out, while she wants a relaxing environment to escape the everyday pressures of parenting and working, as well as a place for the kids to play. The real issue is that they want a home that will satisfy both of their needs, and that becomes the basis for working together to find a creative solution.

Be Intentional

Diane and I have tried to take a weekend away once every year or so to reevaluate our relationship. We look at all the areas of our life such as the physical, spiritual, financial, emotional, etc. We stay at a hotel somewhere near the beach and walk, talk, think, and dream. It's often hard to make time to do this in our busy schedules, but that focused time provides great rewards.

The first time we went away, I thought we were just going to talk. But Diane had prepared a written agenda. I wasn't too excited when I saw it, because we obviously had different expectations of what that weekend would look like. So we worked together to revise the agenda to meet both of our needs. We still followed the topics, but we added times for coffee shops, walking, and relaxing together.

During those weekends, we make sure we come up with simple, specific steps to take that are easily manageable. For instance, it's not effective to say, "I'm going to get in shape this year." (There are lots of shapes.) It's more effective to say, "I'm going to walk around the park three times each week and go to the gym twice a week."

Those weekends have turned out to be one of the most important events in our year. They keep us connected around our common purpose—the health and growth of our relationship.

Plan Backward

One of the effective principles of project management is planning backward. Most people ask, "What should we do first? What should we do next?" A better way is to make sure there's a firm date for the outcome and then ask, "What's the last thing that needs to be done in order to reach our goal—and when does it need to happen?" Working backward provides a much more realistic approach to scheduling and allows for realistic planning for dealing with the unexpected.

A good question to ask is, "Where do I want to be a year from now, ten years from now, when I'm in my senior years?" That question can apply to any relationship, whether personal or professional. If we know what we want our relationships to be like in ten years, we can decide where we want to be in five years—then one year. That helps us decide what we should do today and tomorrow to get there.

Schedule Check-in Sessions

One of the best ways to prevent people problems on the journey toward our destination is to have sessions to check in with each other. This isn't a time for nagging or fault finding; it's simply a chance to talk about how things went regarding the commitments we made last week and decide what we'll do in the next week. These short sessions can be scheduled on a Saturday morning or evening and keep issues from escalating or being ignored. When we don't talk about issues, our relationships can lose momentum.

Act Daily

At the beginning of every day, we should ask ourselves one question: "What one thing will I do today to move our relationship ahead?" It doesn't have to be big—just important. Tiny steps done consistently over a long period of time lead to huge results.

Having a sense of purpose in a relationship won't cure every problem. But when conversations get tough, that sense of purpose provides the security and motivation for us to make it to our destination.

We need to decide where Paris is for our most important relationships—and why we want to go there in the first place. The better the destination, the more motivated we'll be to get there.

Tips for Tough Conversations

To make sure we keep talking when conversations get tough, we need a destination that's worth going to. A destination provides the momentum for us to get through the hard times. If the destination is worthy enough, the tough conversations are worth the effort.

- Decide on the purpose of every relationship we have.
- Determine what it will take to achieve that purpose.
- Use that purpose to keep us on track when the conversational challenges come.

Growing into Connection

We've got the tools in our toolbox. We're developing the skills to use those tools effectively. As we hone our skills and sharpen our tools, there are three more questions to consider:

1. How does all this apply to families, where those tough conversations tend to surface more frequently?
2. Is there anything we can do to keep conversations from getting tough in the first place?
3. How can we use technology as a communication tool and not let it interfere in our relationships in the future?

This is a journey worth taking, because our key relationships are at stake. In this final section, let's fine-tune the process.

16

Relating to Relatives

Happiness is having a large, loving, caring, close-knit family . . . in another city.

George Burns[1]

"Your kids are perfect," we'd often hear from their friends' parents. "They're so polite and well-behaved. You must be so proud!"

We were thinking, *Whose kids are they talking about?* Our kids were awesome and still are. But parents see their kids at their best and at their worst. When they're visiting others, they often want to make a good impression. At home, they relax. We see their good side, but we also see the relaxed side. It's not always pretty.

We often tend to be nicer to strangers than to the people we live with. We're polite. We talk to them about what's happening in their lives. If they've invited us over for dinner, we might bring a small gift. Even if we don't care for what they serve, we eat it anyway and compliment them on the meal. The next day we send them a simple thank-you note, text, or email telling them what a great time we had.

These are common courtesies. We treat people with respect not because they're perfect but because they're human. We're just exercising the Golden Rule: "Do to others what you would have them do to you" (Matt. 7:12 NIV). This is how people live and work well together in society.

When it comes to family, we sometimes forget the Golden Rule. We rewrite it to read, "Do unto others as we think they deserve."

When the Honeymoon Is Over

Everything new goes through a honeymoon period. Whether a new relationship, a new job, a new house, or a new car, it starts with excitement. But over time, the newness wears off. The new car smell is gone, and there's a rattle we can't identify. The new job becomes mundane, the new house gets dirty, and the new relationships get comfortable. In all cases, there's a temptation to turn it in for a newer model.

"New" is good and exciting in a relationship. But when the honeymoon is over, we need a level of commitment to maintain the relationship. We tend to take our relationships for granted when they become comfortable. Comfort is good, because it allows us to relax and be ourselves. But even in the midst of that comfort, we need to treat each other with civility and respect.

What would it be like if we went to someone's home for dinner and acted the way we sometimes do in our own house? We might walk in without greeting the host, plop down on a chair, and say, "What's for dinner?" We might complain about our day, talk about how tired we are, and tell them all the things that went wrong. We might focus on our problems and never ask about theirs. If we don't like the dinner, we might say, "I guess your oven timer isn't working, right?" We leave without saying thank you and show up unannounced the next day to go through the process again.

Sure, we're tired at the end of the day. Whether we were in a corporate setting, working from a home office, or running a household, we used up a lot of energy. It's easy to take family members for granted because they're probably not going anywhere. Customers do business somewhere else if we don't treat them well, but family members tend to stick around anyway.

I heard a psychologist say years ago that after listening to people all day long, the last thing he wanted to do was help his sixth-grade daughter with her math. But when he pulled in the driveway at the end of the day, he would shut off the engine and sit quietly for a few moments before going in the house. He would remind himself that he was about to do the most important work of his day with the most important people in his life.

If we take family members for granted, they may not move away physically—but they move away emotionally. We need a place to be ourselves and to be comfortable, a place to relax and unwind. But the other people in our house need the same thing. The family needs to be comfortable for them, not just us.

Before my wife and I were married, we went through premarital counseling. There was one phrase the counselor used repeatedly that stuck in our minds: "Home should be a place with open arms and bread in the oven." His point was that the goal of our relationship was to make a place of safety when the rest of the world felt unsafe. Some people might interpret it in terms of roles, where one person is out working while the other is home making dinner. But that's not the point. The point is that everyone needs to know, while they can get beat up in the world, they can come home, where they know they're loved (open arms) and their basic needs will be met (warm bread in the oven).

This sense of safety doesn't mean there will never be strong emotions or tough conversations. But we will have created a place of unconditional acceptance where people value each other and treat each other with respect. If we can build our home into a place of safety and honesty, it becomes a place where honest, tough conversations can take place.

That's the goal. No family is perfect, and we all have plenty of room to grow. The most dysfunctional family situation might seem hopeless, and we might need professional help to start building those safety systems. But we can still begin treating others in our family with respect, no matter how they treat us. We might need tough conversations, but when we conduct them with respect, we can begin influencing others. If we do the maintenance ourselves and practice the Golden Rule, we'll begin influencing those important relationships—no matter how unhealthy they are right now.

"But What if They Don't Cooperate?"

After I wrote *People Can't Drive You Crazy if You Don't Give Them the Keys*,[2] most people told me that their biggest aha from the book was that we can't fix other people. If our happiness depends on how another person behaves, we'll spend most of our lives frustrated. Freedom comes when we work on the one person we have control over: ourselves. I'm responsible for what I do, not for what you do.

We can't force people to change, but we can influence them. How? By changing ourselves. When we change, others tend to react differently to us, either positively or negatively.

Let's say I get irritated with you, but I don't say anything. Every time you say something, I respond with sarcastic, cutting remarks. At first, they might seem like casual comments. But over time, you get tired of them. You try to get me to stop, but

I keep going. You feel attacked and eventually build up a wall between us because you have to protect yourself from getting hurt.

I respond negatively because it's painful to live with a barrier between us. I start getting bitter toward you because you never listen. I begin to nag you about your need to change. That makes the situation worse, because you're focused on my need to change. We both feel hopeless, because we assume there's no hope for anything getting better until the other person changes. So the wall gets taller and thicker, and we continue to reinforce it.

One day, I realize that I'm playing a big part in the problem. Instead of waiting for you to make the first move, I decide to stop making sarcastic responses. I consciously determine to think about each thing I say before I say it. I learn to honestly express my feelings in a way that isn't mean or degrading to you.

Are you going to be suspicious? Absolutely. You'll wonder what I'm up to, what my underlying motive is, or how long this new approach will last. But if that approach continues over time, you'll start to believe I've changed. There's no guarantee you'll come around, because the damage already done to the relationship might be deep. But you'll feel less of a need to lash out because I've taken the pressure off.

My motives in changing have to be genuine, though. I can't simply pretend to be nicer while avoiding the real issues, hoping you'll respond differently. Fake sincerity shows through over time, especially because you'll be looking for it. I need to treat you with respect because it's the right thing to do, no matter how you respond. If my personal happiness and comfort are dependent on you, I've given away control over my emotions.

Here's the bottom line: if I genuinely change, there's a good chance you'll change in response. But the only way to begin healing is to work on me, not you. My behavior is the only place I can truly make a difference.

Handling the Herd

One-on-one relationships can be challenging, but things get even tougher when relatives get together. Family gatherings tend to bring out both the best and the worst in people, especially at holidays. We often have expectations that our holidays will look like a Thomas Kinkade painting, with doves cooing on the windowsill and everyone sipping apple cider while they laugh warmly at funny stories. We know better, but we've seen enough Hallmark commercials to make us hopeful.

Reality sets in pretty quickly during those family events. In a dysfunctional family, everyone is talking, nobody is listening, and everybody is waiting to see where the first confrontation will take place. In a functional family, there's a foundation of trust. But every family has a stray family member or two who puts everyone on edge. The best celebrations have the potential to fall apart when expectations are high and communication skills are lacking.

Most of us love the music, the lights, and the decorations of holidays and special events. But on the day the family gathers, we stress about the event, and our emotions can be wrung out for days afterward. How can we enjoy the celebration?

- *We give up expectations for the day.* If we believe everything will run smoothly, we'll set ourselves up for disappointment. It's better to have *expectancy*, which means we have no idea what's going to happen, but we approach the day as an adventure. That doesn't mean it will be perfect, but we'll be ready for the surprises.

- *We don't try to fix people during the event.* Unhealthy people have been that way for a long time. If they try to hijack the celebration, it can turn into an ugly scene. Our tendency is to ask, "What's wrong with you?" and then critique their approach to life and how it impacts others. That's a conversation for another time, not during the event. We're better off pulling them aside and dealing with their immediate behavior, not trying to fix their character.

- *We set boundaries.* We need to decide ahead of time what boundaries we need in order to enjoy the day. If we work best in the kitchen alone, we don't want to wait until we're frustrated by the crowd that gathers. It's better to tell everyone, "I'm going to spend the next forty-five minutes getting things ready in the kitchen while you guys hang out in the den. Then I'll ask for volunteers to help me set the table." We don't have to be a dictator, but we can create some structure for our own sanity.

- *We give ourselves space if we need it.* The day starts early and runs late and is filled with nonstop commotion. That's like driving at high speed without taking a break. When there's potential for conflict during the day (no matter how small), we need to have our emotional reserves in place. It's valuable (especially for introverts) to take small breaks to maintain our energy—like a few minutes alone in our room or a short walk alone or with one other person. If people ask where we're going, we can be honest: "I'm just getting a little space. I'll be back in ten."

- *We focus on individuals.* It's easy to see a crowd of people and miss the joy of individual relationships. When there's a family member who tends to bring stress to the occasion, people tend to avoid them. But taking time to sit with them and simply have a meaningful conversation, practicing the Golden Rule, can diffuse the energy that gets spread over the group. Whether we're the host or just attending, we need a few undistracted conversations with the people we care about the most as well as the ones who challenge us the most.

- *We respond rather than react.* When someone becomes negative, we need to choose how we're going to respond instead of reacting impulsively. The healthy way of handling snarky comments is to take a few seconds to think, "Okay, I know what I feel like saying. Is that really the best thing to say in this situation?" Then we can choose the best way to respond.

The Reality of Bandwidth

I'm always amazed at people who have to rent an auditorium or a park for their family reunion. They might have one hundred people or more coming, and coordinating the event is like putting on a major conference.

My family isn't that big. Our last (and only) family reunion happened at my brother's house and consisted of my brother, my sister, and myself. Three people. We considered using name tags with our pictures on them but decided they would raise the cost of the event too much. (Attendance would have quadrupled if our spouses and kids had been there.)

No matter how big a family is, there's not enough time to give everyone the same amount of attention. That's tough, because many people feel the need to treat every member equally. "After all, they're family. Don't they deserve to get our best attention?"

Actually, no. We have only so much time and energy, and we need to budget where we invest them. When we spend time with one person, we are automatically not spending that time with anyone else. This doesn't mean some people are more important or valuable than others. It means we don't want to shortchange our key relationships for the sake of the peripheral ones.

It's a matter of bandwidth. An internet connection with low bandwidth is like a small-diameter garden hose. Only so much water (data) can go through it at one time. A bigger garden hose can handle more water at a time, and a bigger internet connection can handle more data at a time.

We have a limited bandwidth for relationships. That's why we can't meet everyone's needs. Strange as it sounds, we need to prioritize our relationships. We need to decide which family members get the most attention and which ones get the least, not because some are more valuable but because we don't want to shortchange the people in our lives we have the most commitment to.

I think of my family as a series of concentric circles—a target. The inner circles represent my immediate family relationships. For me, that means my wife gets top priority. She's in the bull's-eye of my personal radar, which means she'll always get more attention than anyone else. If I want my marriage to last a long time, I need to invest the time and energy in it to make that happen.

My kids are next. They have their own lives and families, but I want to invest in those relationships because they're permanent relationships. My grandkids are part of that circle, because grandparents have the opportunity to build different things into their grandkids' lives than their parents can. I'm committed to them for life.

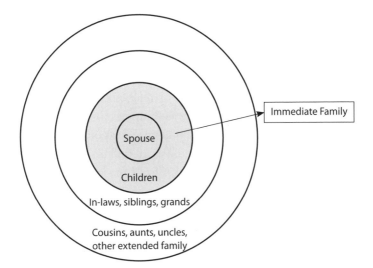

As the circles expand away from the center, they include in-laws, siblings, and other extended family. I value those relationships greatly and become closer to some of those people than others. I invest in those relationships but not at the expense of the inner circles.

When my bandwidth reaches capacity, I don't want to sacrifice the inner circles for the outer circles. My energy always gets focused from the inside out.

Sometimes the outer circles provide less drama than the inner circles because I don't see those people as often. It's easy to gravitate toward them, because they're easier and more fun when tough things are happening in the inner circles. That's when I need to reaffirm my commitment to the valuable relationships in the center, giving them the focus and energy they deserve.

Staying Focused

The key to effective family relationships is to be intentional about them. It's easy to take them for granted and ignore the maintenance. But the more value something has, the more it needs to be taken care of.

Family provides the greatest opportunity for pleasure or pain. In healthy relationships, there will be a good helping of both.

Marriage vows promise commitment "for better or for worse." Can we adapt that mind-set to all our family members? Certainly. We don't wait for them to change before we treat them with respect. It's something we do, regardless of what they do.

We can't change our relatives. We can only change ourselves and then see how others respond. That's the key to thriving in a family.

17

Rust-Free Relationships

Have a heart that never hardens, and a temper that
never tires, and a touch that never hurts.

Charles Dickens[1]

Growing up in Arizona, I remember seeing classified ads for
used cars. Many times the ad would include the words,
"Always in Phoenix." I didn't understand why that was important, so I asked my dad.

"It's because cars don't last very long in other parts of the
country," he said. "When there's ice on the road, they spread salt
to melt it. When that salty slush gets splashed up under the car,
the body rusts. But in Phoenix, there's no ice—so there's no salt,
so there's no rust. Cars don't last as long when they start to rust."

Now we live in Southern California, so we still don't have
rust on our cars. But if I leave tools outside, they get rusty. At
first, the finish begins to fade. Then the rust begins to appear.
Once it does, the tools begin to wear out more quickly. I can
clean the rust off with steel wool and oil, but I can still see the

205

damage that's been done. If the rust is left long enough, the metal loses its integrity and breaks.

It's a lot easier to keep the rust off in the first place. The more valuable the tool is, the more important it is to maintain it.

The Science of Relationships

The Second Law of Thermodynamics says that when left alone, things tend to slow down, not speed up. That means that if we shove a shopping cart across a level parking lot, the cart will slow down and eventually stop (usually when it hits our own car door). The only way the cart will keep moving is if we keep pushing it.

That's true of relationships as well. A good one doesn't stay good all by itself. If we neglect it by not investing in it or putting energy into it, it will slow down and come to a stop. Even the best relationships will end if we take them for granted. The more valuable the relationship, the more important it is to take care of it.

This is true of every type of relationship. As we discussed in the previous chapter, we need to prioritize our relationships to fit the time we have available. That's why we can't ignore our marriages, our relationships with our kids, or our closest business relationships. If we take a spouse, teenager, or boss for granted, there can be serious consequences. We can't allow a casual friend or a connection on social media to capture time that deserves to go to one of these important relationships.

Healthy relationships have the strength to handle the hard work of tough conversations. They're able to handle it because they've been well maintained during the easy times.

How to Prevent Rust

Think of our relationships as valuable tools. We don't buy tools to display them; we buy tools to use them to accomplish something. If maintained, they have the potential to last a long time and make a real difference.

Here are four ways to keep our relationships healthy and rust-free.

Become a Student of the Other Person

When I purchased my current smartphone, I bought a book that went into the details of how to use it. For a long time, I just knew the basics: how to connect to my email, go online, set alarms, send texts, and download apps. I was happy, because I knew the phone would do a lot of really cool things. I even discovered that I could make phone calls on it—an added bonus. Eventually, I became comfortable with the phone. The newness wore off, but I knew how to do the basics.

Sometime later, I picked up the book and began going through it. I would read a couple of pages to learn something new and then would try it out on the phone. I'm still trying to learn one new thing each day. The more I learn about the phone, the more satisfied and excited I am. The more I learn and implement, the more I regain the excitement I had when it was new.

Relationships have the potential to grow exponentially because our lives are a never-ending reservoir of uniqueness. If we make it our goal to explore, study, and learn new things about each other, our excitement can grow toward its potential. We won't be looking for shiny new relationships because we've invested so much in those we have—and there's so much more to explore and learn.

Don't Get Used to the Rust

I had a friend who bought a house in Torrance, California, with a railroad track literally outside his back fence. The train would come barreling through about five or six times each night. For the first few months, he barely slept (but realized why the house was so cheap). But within six months, he didn't even notice it.

He'd have friends over for dinner, and they would ask, "How can you stand it?"

He would reply, "Stand what?"

If we live with the abnormal long enough, it becomes normal.

Every time we purchased a house over the years, we did a walk-through before signing the final paperwork. We saw many things wrong that we were committed to changing: "Those baseboards are so seventies—we need to replace them right away." "Those hinges are rusty—they have to go." "The garage door barely works. It could be dangerous, so we need to replace it."

But after we moved in, we'd have to go back to work, and life would take over. All those things we were so anxious to take care of didn't seem quite as pressing anymore, and we soon forgot about them. They're still there. But we've gotten used to them. We don't notice them anymore.

The longer relationships last, the more comfortable we get. Comfort is a great thing, unless we start taking a relationship for granted. We get used to communication patterns that really need some attention, but it's easier to just slide them into the background. We need to be intentional about those issues, making sure we don't get used to them.

It can be fun and exciting to use a new tool or appliance. We see the results right away, and we're pleased with what the tool or gadget enables us to do. But maintenance isn't fun and exciting. It takes time to clean up a tool after using it, and we don't see anything significant from our effort. The payoff is big, but we don't see it immediately.

The same is true in the fire service. Fighting a fire is a high-energy activity with lots of adrenaline. Preventing fires is a low-energy activity that might seem mundane, but it produces huge results over time.

Relationships are exciting when we have those high-energy encounters that keep things moving. Routine or tough conversations aren't as exciting, but they're an important part of the maintenance that leads to healthy, long-lasting connections. It's energizing to talk when things are going well. It's draining to talk when they're not going well. Talking during both times is essential if a relationship is going to endure and mature. Strong relationships come from doing the routine maintenance.

Deal with Rust Quickly

Last week during a routine exam, my dermatologist did a biopsy on a suspicious spot he found on my ear. If it turns out to be cancerous, he'll be doing surgery. I said, "Am I going to be like one of those guys I've seen in your waiting room with half their ear missing because of surgery?"

"No," he replied. "Not at this stage. But if you waited another seven years before coming to see me, you'd be one of those guys."

When we identify small things in our relationships that need attention, we need to deal with them quickly so we don't have to do extensive surgery later.

King Solomon said, "Catch the foxes for us, the little foxes that are ruining the vineyards, while our vineyards are in blossom" (Song of Sol. 2:15 NASB). The little foxes do damage. If we catch them when they're little, we won't have to deal with them when they're big.

Check for Rust Often

When we're busy with crazy co-workers, demanding toddlers, needy spouses, nosy neighbors, and a perpetual pile of laundry, we get tired. The pressures of life suck us dry, and we don't have energy for routine maintenance. If the wheels of a relationship aren't falling off, we figure we can deal with it later. When that happens, our focus gets distracted from important issues to urgent issues. That's when it's time to develop a routine of maintenance so we don't have to think about it.

Messages come up on my car's dashboard so I don't have to think about maintenance all the time. My car automatically reminds me when something needs to be done. We need to have the same reminders in our relationships. We can put coffee, lunch, or dinner on the calendar regularly to check in with each other. We can use a simple "start, stop, continue" agenda to discover issues while they're small:

- What are we not doing that we need to *start* doing?
- What are we doing that we need to *stop* doing?
- What are we doing that's working and we need to *continue* doing?

Simple, monthly checkups keep things from building up over time. They prevent the heated outbursts that happen when little things are allowed to grow into big things.

A Risky Exercise

I heard someone suggest a challenge for becoming a better partner in any relationship. In a neutral, nonemotional setting, ask the following question: "On a scale of 1 to 10, how would you rate me as a (husband, wife, friend, boss, sibling, etc.), and what would it take to move me up to a 10?"

That's a risky exercise, and one that might not be practical in a damaged, low-trust relationship. But this is a chapter about maintenance, not repair. So we're assuming we have a healthy relationship that we want to keep that way.

If that's true, we might consider trying this exercise. The key is to listen without explaining or becoming defensive. We're just looking for honest input, and we won't get it if we don't make the situation safe for them to talk. We can ask the question, give them time to think (several days if necessary), thank them for their input, and take time to process. Then we can wait a few days or weeks to respond but only with what we plan to change based on what they said.

This is a great way to show people that we honestly value their perspective.

It's also a great way to avoid rusty relationships.

18

Redeeming Technology

Dance like no one is watching . . . because they're not . . . they are checking their phone.

Anonymous

You're going on a long-awaited vacation, and you're at the airport. It's close to boarding time, and you reach for your cell phone. It's not in your pocket. You check your other pockets and your bag and then realize you left it in the car in the airport parking lot. You could go back and get it, but you'd have to go through security again and might miss your flight. What would you do?

A few years ago, this wouldn't have been an issue. We had a cell phone we used only for calls or emergencies. If we forgot it, we could use a pay phone. But now, our phones have become our connection to the world.

Suppose you decide not to go back to get your phone. What would you miss by not having it? Sure, you wouldn't have the security of instant access or emergency help when needed. If you're using it as your camera, you could buy a cheap one on the trip. You would have to check flight status or weather another way, but you could do it.

There are other things our phones will do, but they're not essential. We've just become accustomed to 24/7 access. Imagine what a vacation would be like if we couldn't access social media, search engines, or texting.

We might have to talk to each other.

How Our Lives Have Changed

How do we tell our teenagers that it's time for dinner?

A few years ago, we simply yelled up the stairs, "Dinner's ready!" If they didn't come down right away, we walked upstairs to their room to get their attention. Maybe their music was too loud, or they were on the phone—or maybe they were just being teenagers.

Now it's different. One mom said, "I just text them. They are always in their rooms with their headphones on, listening to music or playing a video game. They wouldn't hear me if I yelled. But I know that texting is a sure way of getting their attention. They never miss a text."

Sound familiar? Here are some other scenarios we've all seen:

- a spouse who seems addicted to his phone, pulling it out whenever there's a lull in the conversation
- kids playing video games for hours on end while their bicycles sit idle in the garage
- a family sitting around the dinner table with each person tethered to something electronic
- a television that provides constant background noise, whether people are watching it or not

- a person trying to start a conversation with someone who's on their laptop or tablet and can't be pulled away

We all need and want healthy relationships, and we value the simple conversations that make those relationships happen. When those relationships are healthy, they can be the most satisfying things we have in life. When they're unhealthy, they cause great pain—because they're keeping us from the connection we inwardly crave.

We don't teach newborn babies how to drive a car, balance a checkbook, or decorate a room. But we teach them to communicate. They can make it through life without learning to drive, but communication is the most basic skill they'll use every day of their lives. We'd call it a "survival skill." The better they become at communication, the more effective their lives will be.

Some people assume that technology is the enemy because it's robbing people of their conversational skills. This isn't really a new argument. Throughout history, people complained about any tool that was different from what they were used to:

- Books were boycotted because they let people gain knowledge in unacceptable ways.
- When the phone rang (on the wall), everybody ran to answer it. It was unheard of to just let it ring. Family members started talking to others on the phone instead of to each other in their home.
- In the 1960s, kids began walking around with transistor radios held to their ears, and people complained that doing so distracted them from normal conversations.
- Television was criticized because people were just passively entertained every evening.

But in each case, the benefits eventually outweighed the criticism. People found ways to use these tools to connect more effectively. Tools keep changing, and the benefits keep growing. But so do the numbers of people who complain about them.

A friend told me that when he was growing up, his grandpa used his grandma as the television remote control. "Go change the channel," he'd say—and she would get up and change it. She had to physically turn a knob on the set to get a different show.

We had next-door neighbors who were much more sophisticated. They had a device that attached to the knob on the television with a long cable that reached across the room to the couch. There was an identical knob at the other end. When they turned that knob, it turned the knob on the set across the room. We were stunned. We didn't know technology like that existed.

The Downside of Technology

In the past, if we were standing in line at the post office, we had two options:

1. Talk to someone.
2. Think.

I'm writing this paragraph at a Starbucks. There are thirteen people in line. Eleven of them are looking at their phones. I'm guessing that if the other two people tried to strike up a conversation with one of them, those people would think, *Can't you see I'm busy?* I'm not faulting them. If I were on my phone in that line, I'd probably have the same reaction.

One of the biggest areas in which technology has made an impact is in the way we communicate with each other.

One human resource manager described her frustration to me recently. "The biggest problem I run into is people who don't know how to interview for a job. They have great degrees and great skills from great schools, but they don't know how to have a conversation. They rarely make eye contact, and they don't know how to engage with me when we're talking. In fact," she went on, "I was interviewing someone last week who interrupted me because he wanted to respond to a text he had just received."

"What did you do?" I asked.

"I let him step outside to handle his text. Then I locked the door."

There's a risk here. It's easy for the older generation to criticize the younger generation when these communication issues bubble up to the surface. "They spend so much time on their electronic stuff that they don't know how to have a conversation. All they do is play games and work on getting high scores."

Maybe that's true. An older man I talked to yesterday described walking out of his house on Christmas Day and finding the street empty. "A few years ago, you'd see kids everywhere trying out their new bikes and skateboards," he said. "But this year, the street was empty. Not a single kid anywhere. I'm sure they were all inside playing with their latest electronic toy."

But adults aren't innocent. Maybe they're not playing video games or spending hours on social media. But how often do they reach for their smartphone to check their email during a meal? They might not be addicted to drugs or alcohol, but they've developed a new kind of addiction: technology.

In other words, we're misusing a great tool. Technology is an awesome resource to *enhance* our conversations. It was never designed to *replace* them.

The Need for a Strategy

The good news? Because of technology, life is much easier. Information is available instantly without a trip to the library, and we can access it in our jammies.

The bad news? Because of technology, life is much harder. There's so much information available that we get overwhelmed and want to spend the day in our jammies.

We need an action plan—an intentional, carefully crafted approach to technology. The plan starts with us making sure we discover ways to control it in our own lives.

Then we make a plan with the people in our lives. We focus on the common goals we have in our most important relationships, build the foundations we've discussed in this book to make them honest and effective, and design a technology plan that works for that relationship. Simply stated, technology should make our relationships better.

Sharing words in print is a form of communication, but it doesn't convey the emotion that comes through tone of voice, facial expression, and body language. Written words can't hold or hug. Written words can't listen or make eye contact. A friend once told his aging grandmother, "Because you listened to me, I knew you loved me. And because you loved me, I listened to you."

Younger people might be challenged in their conversational skills because they haven't had the practice that develops the muscle memory for the give-and-take of conversations. When we have live conversations over a lifetime, we develop patterns of interaction that build human moments. We learn to value the uniqueness of others—learning that they don't think like us, and that's okay. We grow from valuing the differences in others instead of feeling the need to change them.

A Fifteen-Million-Dollar Dinner Bell

The basic principle is simple. Technology is a tool. If we learn to control it, it will serve us well.

It's a lot easier to learn how to use our tools well than to get rid of them and do everything manually. (I've tried changing a tire with just my hands, and it didn't go well trying to get the lug nuts off.) We can actually learn to love technology for what it can do instead of resisting it.

Early in our marriage, we lived a few miles from Luke Air Force Base outside of Phoenix. A man who lived a few houses away was a helicopter pilot in the Air Force and went on military maneuvers around the state every day. He had fairly normal working hours and usually came home for dinner each night. But he never knew exactly when that would be, so his wife never knew when to have dinner ready.

He used technology to create a solution. On his flight back to the base each night, he would make his final approach to the base as low as possible over his house. His wife would hear his fifteen-million-dollar aircraft overhead and know he would walk in the door twenty-eight minutes later.

Now that's a creative use of technology.

When Conversations Get Challenging

Several years ago, I wrote *How to Communicate with Confidence*[1] to provide tools and techniques for negotiating everyday conversations. This is an area in which many people struggle, especially those who are introverted.

When relationships advance and conversations get tough, a different set of tools and techniques is needed. The basics are still required, but the stakes are higher. For critical conversations, we need to kick our skills up to the next level.

The problem? We can't text a tough conversation. The more that's at stake, the more critical it is to connect in person. That's threatening for many of us, so we try to avoid conflict by sending our thoughts electronically. Doing so feels safer somehow, because we don't have to see the other person's reaction. We don't have to negotiate their emotions. But without the 93 percent of communication that takes place in person, putting confrontation in writing can be like pouring gasoline onto a quickly spreading blaze.

High emotion, high value, and low communication make the perfect storm. They're a recipe for disaster.

Reading the Safety Instructions

It's dangerous to write anything about technology in a book. Whatever is happening today will be obsolete by the time you read this. So we can't discuss any one form of technology. Instead, we need to craft an approach to technology that works no matter how it changes. That way we'll be ready when those changes take place. We can see technology for what it actually is—a tool to enhance our relationships, not to replace them. When we have that perspective, we'll be prepared to use technology effectively rather than being used by it.

That's what tools are for. I have a chain saw, for instance. It saves me a lot of time when I'm trimming trees. But if I don't respect that tool, it can be dangerous. That's why the first third of the instruction manual is about how to keep the saw from hurting me. I've learned to follow those safety procedures, and the saw does an amazing job.

Our technology is the same way. It can provide some amazing benefits for our relationships and our communication:

- We have instant access to others.
- We can find information to make our conversations accurate.
- We can keep up with more people in less time.
- We can stay connected easily when we're apart.

But if we don't recognize that it can also do damage, we're setting ourselves up to be victims of that technology.

Technology isn't the enemy; it's just a tool. Whether it's positive or negative depends on how we use it. It's like a razor-sharp scalpel. In the hands of a skilled surgeon, it's good. In the hands of a crazed criminal, it's bad.

We will always have relationships. Technology isn't going anywhere either. The key is figuring out how to get them to work together. It's like two porcupines that fall in love. They need each other but have to learn how to keep from sticking each other and causing pain.

Twenty Ways to Make Technology Our Friend

Most of us don't have helicopters at our disposal. But we have other tools available that often irritate the people we're in relationships with when misused. We need to get creative to find ways to put them to good use.

Here's a short list of ideas, specifically for families (though they can be adapted to other relationships). We can start with a few of these and then work with the other people in our relationships to create other suggestions.

1. Every Sunday, we can decide when during the week we're going to invest in our most important relationships (personal and professional) and in what way. Then we schedule appointments on our calendar to make it happen and honor them as carefully as we would any other appointment.
2. Guys won't ask for directions when driving. But they'll use a GPS or a phone app to find their way around because it's cool. If we encourage their use of technology, we'll get places faster.
3. Don't videotape every moment of our kids' birthday parties and holiday celebrations. When we're behind the camera, we miss the moments. We'll revisit the memories more often than we revisit the recordings.

4. Get a digital video recorder for the television if we don't have one. Then when asked to change the baby, we can use the pause feature instead of saying, "Wait until the next commercial."

5. Set up no-tech zones in the house, like a living room or family room where no electronics are allowed. This becomes a talking/playing/connecting area.

6. Use an app that shows selected people our exact location. My wife and I use it so we know where the other person is if they're running late instead of always having to call. I also have a couple of friends who travel as much as I do for business, and we keep track of each other's locations during trips as a tool for personal integrity and accountability.

7. Use a Bluetooth or similar feature in our car to connect with our spouse on the way home. My friend calls his wife, and they talk about their day so they're connected before he gets home. That frees him up to come home and immediately take over with the kids because he and his wife have already made their initial connection.

8. Have no-tech meals as a family. But put a time limit on it so people don't feel trapped. Let the family decide on the time frame that's realistic. One family turns on the out of office message on their phones at dinnertime. The message says, "Thanks for calling. I'm having dinner with my family right now but will call you back in about thirty minutes when we're done."

9. Develop a family purpose statement, describing what the governing values of the family are. What are the non-negotiables that make the family work? Craft it as a family, put it in writing, and post it in an obvious place. It becomes a personal constitution to help family members evaluate decisions about technology.

10. On trips, come up with a way to utilize technology without letting the kids watch videos the entire journey. Let them come up with ideas for ways to stay busy and entertained, with technology being an essential (but not the only) part. Get their input for ideas so they have some ownership.

11. Come up with projects that will involve using technology in a positive way. An example would be to give a teenager an electronic reading device after they've read fifty paper books from the library. Then teach them how to download library books for free on their device.

12. Develop a culture of playing board games as a family. Make sure the games are age appropriate and fun and invite their friends to be part of the festivities. Board games won't replace their tech games, but they will provide a chance for nonelectronic entertainment that includes personal interaction.

13. Use social media to stay in touch with family and friends and to share photos of important events. If we're not tech savvy, it's worth the investment of time to figure this one out. Our kids can teach us. This is also a way of respecting them by participating in their world.

14. Use texting when we need a quick response from someone. We'll often get it, since most people keep their phone with them constantly. But we shouldn't let texting replace real conversation. If we get to a place where texting with someone becomes more comfortable than meeting with them, there's a problem.

15. Sunday football often interferes with church, and many fans resent the intrusion. So agree on a synergistic solution. Record the game, attend the service, and then watch the game together (or at least give the sports enthusiast genuine freedom to watch it later).

16. Use Skype or other video connections to stay in touch with people in distant locations. It's not as good as being in their presence, but it gives us a chance to see the other person's expressions and hear their tone of voice. My son dated his wife for over five years primarily through Skype when he lived in San Diego and she lived in Guadalajara. Sometimes they would both dress up for their online date and prepare a nice meal (separately). He would buy her flowers to show her on the screen. It was a creative way to stay connected when distance made live connection unrealistic.

17. Leave our phone in the car when having dinner with friends. It speaks volumes to the other people that we think they're important enough for us to be 100 percent undistracted.

18. Find ways to meet each other's needs, letting technology have its proper place. If a wife loves foot rubs, and her husband loves football, he can give her a foot rub while watching the game, and they're both happy.

19. Find a fiction book that the kids are interested in and read a chapter aloud at dinner. If the book is good, they'll look forward to the end of the meal and the next segment.

20. When you see something that you think another person would find exciting or valuable, take a picture of it and text it to them. It's a quick way to let them know you were thinking about them and care about what matters to them.

Take Back Our Relationships

Technology isn't going anywhere. In fact, it's going to increase. That's a good place to start in healing our relationships. We can easily blame technology for the problems in our relationships because we've seen communication erode as technology has grown. It looks like technology is the problem.

But it's not. It's just a tool that has shown up in our lives without an instruction manual. We need to learn how to use it. If I accidently cut myself with a kitchen knife, it doesn't mean that all knives are bad and I should get rid of them. It means I need to learn how to handle knives safely. When that happens, I can do some pretty productive things in the kitchen.

Technology has entered our lives like a raging river after a spring thaw. The river has the potential to be dangerous if not respected, which is why we wouldn't let our toddler play near the banks. But if we harness the power of the river, it can produce electricity for an entire community and provide resources for thousands of people. It doesn't do us any good to be frustrated with the river. We do better to welcome its existence and use it to improve our lives.

In our relationships, it's easy to tell people to get off the phone and communicate. But that ignores the value of the tool. Instead, we need to talk about our common goals and determine how to use technology to help us reach those goals. We always need to see technology as a means to an end, not an end in itself. It exists for something bigger.

So Where Do We Start?

We start with ourselves. We need to analyze how we use technology in our own lives and whether it's helping or hurting us. We need to own up to the addictions we might have to electronic devices. Do we find ourselves compulsively checking email or social media on our phones? If we figure out how to make those tools work for us, we've laid an honest foundation for influencing others.

When we switch from trying to change others to changing ourselves, we've taken the first and biggest step. Changing ourselves is a skill that anyone can learn. When we develop that skill, our influence will grow. As long as we minimize our expectations for others and maximize our expectancy, amazing things can happen in our relationships.

But change doesn't happen overnight. It happens over time. It's a process. If we're at a 3, we can't jump to a 10 overnight. Our goal is to nudge toward a 4. Once we've made it there, we can explore 5 and 6. We need to focus on progress, not perfection.

My wife, Diane, and I have been learning Spanish. We download our lessons, and we listen to each one while we drive or walk. The course manual suggests that we need to feel only about 80 percent comfortable with each lesson before moving on to the next one.

The first couple of lessons were easy, and we felt pretty accomplished at the end. We had hopes of being able to communicate in Spanish someday. Lesson three was more challenging. We had to listen to it several times to make it sink in. Lesson four was even worse. We felt like we would never be able to master the lessons that followed.

But during lesson four, we realized something. We had mastered lessons one and two. They had become second nature. That gave us hope that when we got to five and six, we'd probably have three and four down pat.

Learning to communicate effectively in our most important relationships might seem like trying to empty a swimming pool with a coffee cup. But you're taking the first step by reading this book. The process might seem like it will take forever. The key is to start the journey. Small steps, taken consistently, produce massive results. We're made for relationships. They're worth fighting for.

When tough conversations come, we can approach them with confidence. With the right tools in our toolbox and an understanding of how to apply the right skills, those tough times can be the catalyst to healthy relationships.

Conclusion

You probably picked up this book because you have important relationships in your life and you want to make them better. Maybe the communication has been strained and the conversations have been tough. You're afraid the connection is getting weaker, and you don't want the downward spiral to continue. Or maybe your relationships are great and you just want to keep them that way.

We can't have relationships without real, honest communication. When conversations get tough, we have two main options: engage or disengage. If we engage effectively, communication grows and provides a foundation for the relationship. If we disengage, there's nothing to work on.

That's why we can't text a tough conversation; we have to engage with each other. The danger of technology alone is that it tricks us into thinking we're engaging when we're really disengaging. Electronics send words back and forth, but it's a poor substitute for looking each other in the eyes. If we text instead of talk, it's like walking out the door, glancing back, and saying, "Oh, by the way, I lost our life savings gambling last week."

Technology is an enhancement to our connections, not a substitute. When used effectively, it can be a great add-on for our conversations. But our relationships will grow when we use the tools and practice the skills of effective communication face-to-face. We start by creating safety in a relationship where there's freedom to grow together.

Communication might take time, and it will definitely take work. It's an investment, and the dividends can be huge. There are no guarantees, but it's the best chance we have for a meaningful and satisfying life.

Notes

Introduction: What We've Got Here Is a Failure to Communicate

1. Dr. Albert Mehrabian, *Silent Messages* (Belmont: Wadsworth, 1971).

Chapter 1 How the Elephant Got in the Room

1. "Randy Pausch Quotes," *Goodreads*, accessed March 5, 2015, http://www.good reads.com/quotes/76530-when-there-s-an-elephant-in-the-room-introduce-him.

Chapter 3 What People Need

1. Abraham Maslow, "A Theory of Human Motivation," *Psychological Review* 50 (1943): 370–96.

2. "Max-Neef on Human Needs and Human-scale Development," accessed March 5, 2015, http://www.rainforestinfo.org.au/background/maxneef.htm.

3. Anthony Robbins, "The 6 Human Needs: Why We Do What We Do," *Change Your Life Now*, August 7, 2013, http://training.tonyrobbins.com/the-6 -human-needs-why-we-do-what-we-do/.

Chapter 5 Tool #2—Confidence in Communication (Trust)

1. "The 16 Best Things Warren Buffett Has Ever Said," *Huffington Post*, August 30, 2013, http://www.huffingtonpost.com/2013/08/30/warren-buffett-quotes _n_3842509.html.

Chapter 6 Tool #3—Staying on Your Side of the Checkerboard (Ownership)

1. "Jim Rohn Quotes," *BrainyQuote*, accessed March 5, 2015, http://www.brainy quote.com/quotes/quotes/j/jimrohn133626.html.

Chapter 7 Tool #4—Your Personal Fuel Station (Emotions)

1. Dale Carnegie, *How to Win Friends and Influence People* (New York: Pocket Books, 1981), 14.

Chapter 8 Tool #5—Crock-Pot Relationships (Time)

1. "Famous Quotes by Johann Wolfgang Von Goethe," *Book of Famous Quotes*, accessed April 7, 2015, http://www.famous-quotes.com/author.php?page=12&total=313&aid=2898.
2. "Sistine Chapel Ceiling," *Wikipedia*, accessed March 5, 2015, http://en.wikipedia.org/wiki/Sistine_Chapel_ceiling.

Chapter 10 Skill #1—Make It Safe

1. Lindsey McCready, Johnny Ackley, and Sam Wendler, "Hitchcock Era (30s–60s): History and Psychology," *The Historical Evolution of Fear and Scare Tactics*, accessed March 5, 2015, http://fearincinema.umwblogs.org/hitchcocks/history-psychology/.
2. Joel Gunz, "Enjoyment of Fear/Fear of Enjoyment: Why Hitchcock Makes Me Want to Quit Going to Movies," *Alfred Hitchcock Geek*, October 8, 2005, http://www.alfredhitchcockgeek.com/2005_10_01_archive.html.
3. Ibid.

Chapter 11 Skill #2—Eliminate Intimidation

1. Daniel G. Amen, MD, "ANT Therapy: How to Develop Your Own Internal Anteater to Eradicate Negative Thoughts," American Holistic Health Association, accessed March 5, 2015, http://ahha.org/articles.asp?Id=100.
2. Ibid.

Chapter 12 Skill #3—Practice Power Listening

1. "Margaret Millar Quotes," *BrainyQuote*, accessed March 5, 2015, http://www.brainyquote.com/quotes/quotes/m/margaretmi107912.html.

Chapter 13 Skill #4—Encourage Honest Feedback

1. "'Weekend at Burnsies' Script," *Simpson Crazy*, accessed March 5, 2015, http://www.simpsoncrazy.com/scripts/weekend-at-burnsies.
2. "Ken Blanchard Quotes," *BrainyQuote*, accessed March 5, 2015, http://www.brainyquote.com/quotes/quotes/k/kenblancha204474.html.
3. "The Johari Window: Using Self-Discovery and Communication to Build Trust," *Mind Tools*, accessed March 5, 2015, http://www.mindtools.com/CommSkll/JohariWindow.htm.

Chapter 14 Skill #5—Start with Kindness

1. "Mark Twain Quotes," *BrainyQuote*, accessed March 5, 2015, http://www.brainyquote.com/quotes/quotes/m/marktwain106287.html.

Chapter 15 Skill #6—Know Your Purpose

1. "Benjamin Franklin Quotes," *Goodreads*, accessed March 5, 2015, http://www.goodreads.com/quotes/460142-if-you-fail-to-plan-you-are-planning-to-fail.

2. Harold Kerzner, *Project Management Best Practices: Achieving Global Excellence* (New York: John Wiley & Sons), 370.

Chapter 16 Relating to Relatives

1. "George Burns Quotes," *BrainyQuote*, accessed March 5, 2015, http://www.brainyquote.com/quotes/authors/g/george_burns.html.

2. Mike Bechtle, *People Can't Drive You Crazy if You Don't Give Them the Keys* (Grand Rapids: Revell, 2012).

Chapter 17 Rust-Free Relationships

1. "Charles Dickens Quotes," *Goodreads*, accessed March 5, 2015, http://www.goodreads.com/quotes/28007-have-a-heart-that-never-hardens-and-a-temper-that.

Chapter 18 Redeeming Technology

1. Mike Bechtle, *How to Communicate with Confidence* (Grand Rapids: Revell, 2013).

Mike Bechtle has a unique blend of corporate and ministry experience—from eighteen years in churches and Christian universities to more than three thousand seminars on productivity, leadership, and communication taught to many of the Fortune 500 companies. He is the author of *People Can't Drive You Crazy if You Don't Give Them the Keys* and *How to Communicate with Confidence*; his articles have appeared in publications such as *Writer's Digest*, *Entrepreneur*, *Discipleship Journal*, *Moody*, *Eternity*, and Pastors.com. He has been speaking at corporate events, conventions, and in ministry settings since 1974. After receiving his master's degree at Talbot School of Theology, he received his doctorate in higher and adult education from Arizona State University. Currently a senior training consultant for FranklinCovey Company, he lives in Fullerton, California.

For information about speaking engagements, keynotes, and seminars, visit www.mikebechtle.com.

FOR MORE
COMMUNICATION TOOLS,
PRACTICAL INSIGHT,
AND MOTIVATION VISIT

MIKEBECHTLE.COM
@MIKEBECHTLE

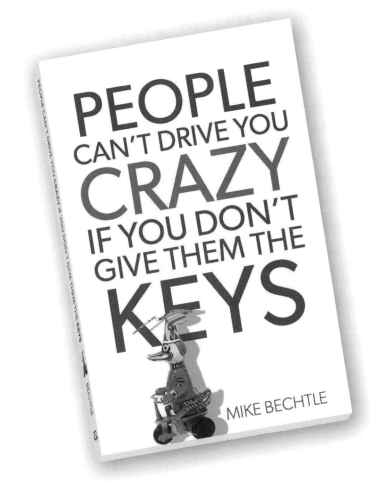

CONFIDENT CONVERSATION
IS EASIER THAN YOU THINK

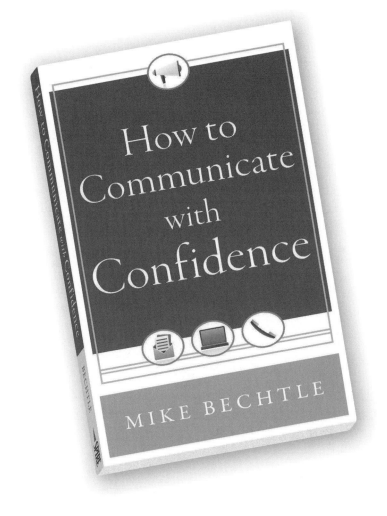

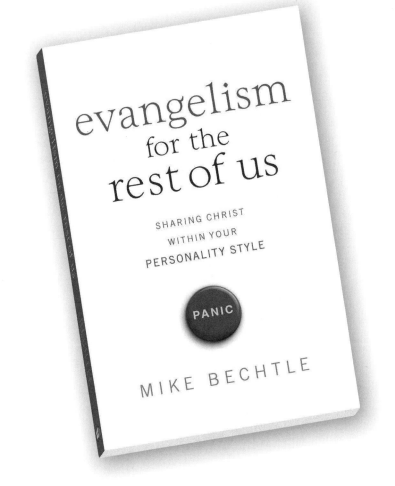